Unveiling Islam

Roger Du Pasquier

Unveiling Islam

Translated from the French by

T. J. WINTER

THE ISLAMIC TEXTS SOCIETY

CAMBRIDGE · 1992

This English edition first published by
The Islamic Texts Society
5 Green Street, Cambridge CB2 3JU, UK

British Library Cataloguing-in-Publication Data
A catalogue record of this book is available from
the British Library

ISBN 0 946621 32 2 *paper*

Typeset by Goodfellow & Egan, Cambridge
Printed by Redwood Press Ltd

Contents

Preface

IN THESE last years of the twentieth century, the world of Islam has captured the attention of the West, and has baffled it. Despite the upheavals brought about by modern civilisation, it has maintained traditional values which the West has deemed obsolete, and remains, in many ways, a world of faith and of prayer.

Even in Europe, where their numbers have reached some fifteen million for the whole continent (if we include Russia west of the Urals), the great majority of Muslims continue to believe. God—*Allah*—is still for them a reality, *the* reality. Many pray regularly.

Overall, it cannot be denied that at a time when all other great religions are in decline—or are at the very least on the defensive—Islam continues to make progress. Africa offers one of the most clear-cut illustrations of this.

This vigour of Islam, contrasted with the ongoing enfeeblement of Christianity, is a major fact of modern history. Many sociological and orientalist studies have already attempted to analyse it, and have pinpointed a number of its trends. But this century, whose civilisation has rejected all transcendence, has failed to comprehend the vitality, even the fervour, of a religion which is essentially transcendent, for its investigative methods are themselves no more than a developed form of secular thought. For Islam *is*, quintessentially, the sacred.

The above remarks indicate the purpose of the present work. Written at the request and under the guidance of Muslim friends who wanted to explain the message of Islam in a form accessible to readers of European background or education, the book conforms to their perspective as believers, not 'observers' or 'experts' who do no more than scrutinise from outside. The reader is thus invited to discover a world still ruled by the sacred, a principle fundamentally alien to modern civilisation, which, in its desire to 'demystify' everything, and by ignoring the vertical dimension of this world, has brought about its desacralisation.

It may be appropriate to point out that to praise the fidelity of those whom Christianity in past centuries believed it could call 'infidels' is in no way a criticism of the Christian religion. In an age in which all revealed religions must struggle against the spirit of negation which is their common enemy, all rivalry between them is senseless.

Islam today cannot be regarded with indifference by anyone who remains alive to the presence, above this fallen world, of a timeless and saving Truth. To unveil Islam as it is is to find proof that this Truth can still be lived, both on the individual and collective levels, wholly and without compromise.

I

The challenge of our time

IT SEEMS that nothing on earth can still escape the crisis which convulses the modern world. To speak of the crisis of a civilisation is not enough, since the phenomenon has assumed universal proportions. The impending darkness draws ever nearer; a sense of disquiet spreads more and more widely.

Islam has been given to man precisely to help him live through this last stage of history without losing himself. The final revelation of the prophetic cycle, it offers methods of resisting the present chaos, and of re-establishing order and clarity within the soul—as well as harmony in human relations—and of achieving the higher destiny to which the Creator has called us.

Islam is addressed to man, of whom it has a deep and precise understanding, defining as it does his position in creation and before God.

Modern thought, by contrast, has no well-defined and generally accepted anthropology. Concerning man it has amassed a vast array of facts, yet the very confusion and variety of these facts betrays an inability to give a coherent definition of the human condition. In no other civilisation has there been such a complete and systematic ignorance of the reason why we are born, why we are alive, and why we must die.

Such is the paradox of our culture, which, in the first place, wishes to be 'humanist'; in other words, to make man the criterion and the end of all things, but in which even the concept of man has broken down. Having been made into a perfected monkey by by evolutionism, he has been relieved of whatever tenuous coherence was left to him by the philosophy of the absurd. The human creature is henceforth to resemble a puppet shaken and disjointed by a mechanism which he himself has set in motion but the chaotic and accelerating movement of which he is no longer able to control.

Proclaimed as absurd, life on earth has effectively lost its meaning. Man is offered a multitude of material possibilities and advantages undreamt of by earlier generations, but, since we are now ignorant of what man is, and of what his deep aspirations might be, not one of these miracles can prevent him from foundering in his own despair.

None the less, modern civilisation has confidently declared that it has brought happiness to the human race. The French Revolution adopted a Declaration of the Rights of Man, and the American constitution claims to assure the 'pursuit of happiness' to every citizen. The nineteenth century sanctioned in every Western country, and even in a few others, the grand idea of Progress by virtue of which the Golden Age lies not behind but before us.

For some time the facts have seemed to confirm this belief. The material conditions of the lower strata of Western society have been greatly improved, individual freedom has been guaranteed to all, science has given man a sense of being incomparably better informed than the greatest sages of past generations, and technological developments have placed tools of a previously unimaginable power in his hands.

On another level, and through psychological theories which claim to have located at last the true centre of gravity of the human being—at the level of sexuality—individuals are promised that they are capable of 'self-fulfillment' simply by throwing off every constraint and following their own inclinations. For many this has been a sufficient excuse to suppress the morality inherited from the past, henceforth to be considered a mass of obsolete prejudices.

In this way, modern man believes that he has come of age, the concomitant assumption being that his forbears of earlier centuries were childish. There is no shortage of philosophers, or even of theologians, to confirm him in this belief.

Yet the facts themselves have at last exploded these theories.

The First World War, and the disasters which it brought in its train, provided a major set-back to the optimism of the heralds of the new golden age. This did not prevent them, however, as soon as peace had returned, from declaiming even more eloquent prophecies of the advent of an era of peace, justice and happiness, as though the monstrous tragedy, with its millions of victims, were no more than a passing aberration.

The Second World War, a still more appalling tragedy, should have revealed to humanity the illusions and dangers of progressist and more or less atheistic ideologies which promise the achievement of happiness through purely profane, quantitative or materialistic means. But instead of discerning their illusory nature, and returning to more spiritual and traditional values, man speeded up the process of secularisation. If the promises of happiness did not come true, then the ideologues of the system never drew the conclusion that they were false or groundless, but instead launched an assault on the last survivals of the old order and of traditional ideas, denouncing them as so many obstacles to the march of progress which must urgently be swept away.

Social upheavals were only one aspect of this trend. They synchronised with a moral and spiritual subversion which, ostensibly, eliminated 'prejudices' and the 'authoritarian' spirit which stood in the way of man's full liberation, and hence his happiness.

The reality, particularly as one can discern it in young people steeped in such 'anti-authoritarian' ideas, is revelatory: according to consistent reports, the number of mental patients and drug addicts continues to mount, paralleling the way in which blind submission to ideological systems and leaders leads in fact to the very antithesis of liberty.

This self-styled 'humanist' civilisation has ended up with a system which both degrades man and deceives him, ultimately to bring about his destruction. It degrades him because it reduces him to the material and quantitative functions of a mere producer and consumer; and it deceives him because it makes him believe that thanks to progress, development, science, better social organisation and liberation from the last 'prejudices' and restraints bequeathed to him by the past, he will some day be received into a state of bliss and triumph over suffering, despite the fact that suffering is intrinsic to the human condition. Finally it destroys him by corrupting him, dividing him within himself, and emptying his life of meaning and of hope.

Moreover, the feeling that the present order of things—if one can speak of order at all amidst such confusion—is a monumental fraud, seems to be spreading steadily, and modern ideologies are increasingly being fought into a corner by a spirit of negation, dissent and nihilism. In effect, these ideologies, including Marxism, always finish by losing their credibility, since they are powerless to answer the most important of our questions about the meaning of our lives and the reason behind our presence here on earth. Ultimately it is inevitable that they become futile and ineffective, since they ignore the fact that man is fundamentally defined through the Absolute, and that at the very bottom of his soul, consciously or otherwise, he seeks for nothing else.

The human condition cannot find its justification and true fulfillment on the horizontal and earthly plane, since it contains an essential and central aspiration towards transcendence. Man, in distinction to other creatures, feels a basic need to reach beyond himself to quest for this Absolute, which, alone among creatures, he is capable of conceptualising. This is why all the relative things which he is offered in such great abundance leave him always hungry, or with a bitter taste in his mouth.

It is deeply significant that the 'counter-culture' should be most developed in the industrialised countries with a high standard of living, where most material goods are within everyone's reach.

This is precisely the point: modern civilisation is unacceptable to man because, in offering him everything except the essential, it seems to him to be devoid of sense. Never before has he had so many ways of distracting himself, and never before has he been so bored. The extraordinary achievements of science and technology, whether in the form of television, the 'conquest of space', or the progress of medicine, have failed to provide any authentic remedy for this *ennui*. Man, amidst this plethora of gadgets, is distracted, diffused or dissipated, but fails to find the true peace of soul which comes from fulfilling in this world the higher destiny for which he was made.

In the senseless conditions of modern life, those who are gifted with some degree of reflectiveness are growing more and more conscious that humanity is rushing towards a precipice. In a perfectly understandable reaction, many search for their salvation beyond the confines of the Western world which has promoted the discredited civilisation. They turn towards various forms of oriental mysticism, such as yoga, or to the occult. But all too often their quest ignores Islam which, nevertheless, would help them to invest their lives with a sense of meaning which answered their most deeply felt aspirations.

Islam is not of the West; yet it cannot be seen as exclusively oriental. Although a stranger to the specifically modern world, it is none the less, of all the sacred traditions, the best adapted to the conditions of the cosmic cycle in its present stage of decline. It is simple and obvious, and yet at the same time holds treasures of mystical and metaphysical wisdom which have provided the nourishment for long generations of contemplatives and saints.

Through its horizontal and vertical dimensions, Islam is capable of reconciling man both with the universe which surrounds him, and with the Creator of all things. In the fullest sense of the term, it is universal.

The West, whether Christian or dechristianised, has never really known Islam. Ever since they watched it appear on the world stage, Christians never ceased to insult and slander it in order to find justifications for waging war on it. It has been subjected to grotesque distortions the traces of which still endure in the European mind. Even today there are many Westerners for whom Islam can be reduced to three ideas: fanaticism, fatalism and polygamy. Of course, there does exist a more cultivated public whose ideas about Islam are less deformed; but there are still precious few who know that the word *islām* signifies nothing other than 'submission to God.' One symptom of this ignorance is the fact that in the imagination of most Europeans, *Allah* refers to the divinity of the Muslims, not the God of the Christians and the Jews; they are all surprised to hear, when one takes the trouble to explain things to them, that '*Allah*' means 'God', and that even Arab Christians know Him by no other name.

Islam has of course been the object of studies by Western orientalists who, over the last two centuries, have published an extensive learned literature on the subject. Nevertheless, however worthy their labours may have been, particularly in the historical and philological fields, they have contributed little to a better understanding of the Muslim religion in the Christian or post-Christian milieu, simply because they have failed to arouse much interest outside their specialised academic circles. One is forced also to concede that Oriental studies in the West have not always been inspired by the purest spirit of scholarly impartiality, and it is hard to deny that some Islamicists and Arabists have worked with the clear intention of belittling Islam and its adherents. This tendency was particularly marked—for obvious reasons—in the heyday of the colonial empires, but it would be an exaggeration to claim that it has vanished without trace.

These are some of the reasons why Islam remains even today so misjudged in the West, where, curiously enough, Asiatic faiths such as Buddhism and Hinduism have for more than a century generated far more visible sympathy and interest, even though Islam is so close to Judaism and Christianity, having flowed from the same Abrahamic source. Despite this, however, for several years it has seemed that external conditions, particularly the growing importance of the Arab-Islamic countries in the world's great political and economic affairs, have served to arouse a growing interest in Islam in the West, resulting—for some—in the discovery of new and hitherto unsuspected horizons.

Islām, which means 'submission to God', expresses a universal idea which one finds in one form or another in the other sacred traditions, for every true religion is necessarily in conformity with the will of the divine Absolute. However, Islam can also be characterised as the 'eternal religion', since, basing itself on the doctrine of Unity, which is eternal, it brings nothing which is fundamentally new; instead it has come to re-establish the primordial religion, and to reaffirm the Truth, which is beyond time.

As a re-establishment and a reaffirmation, Islam is also a synthesis of the universal Revelation: it is the recapitulation of all the previous messages which Heaven has vouchsafed mankind. It is this which gives it its astonishing capacity to integrate, within a single community, believers of very different ethnic origins while respecting their particularities.

Being in essence timeless, Islam is at once ancient and modern. It is ancient because it transmits a truth known to the men of the earliest ages, and it is modern in its methods, which enable people in the present age to live this truth.

This 'modernity' appears firstly in the simplicity of expression of its doctrinal principles, of which the first and the most fundamental is articulated in the *Shahāda* (the confession of faith): *Lā ilāha illa'Llāh, Muḥammadun rasūlu'Llāh* ('there is no deity save God; Muhammad is the messenger of God'). This testimony to the Divine Unity, proclaimed to mankind through the mission of the Prophet Muhammad, is expressed with a clarity which makes it wholly accessible to modern man, who, in order to be Muslim, has no need to subscribe to 'mysteries' impenetrable to his intellect.

Assuredly, the *Shahāda* does have metaphysical implications which human reason may never exhaust, but it none the less brings to man a certainty of the most fundamental kind: that of the divine Absolute made accessible to men by the prophetic message. Islam has justly been described as 'the religion of certainty'.

In this way, the *Shahāda* is Islam's prime response to the promethean agnosticism of today's world. It deploys a fundamental argument which goes beyond the discursive processes of human thought to affirm the absolute Reality on which all created things depend, and of which they are therefore no more than relative expressions. Starting with a negation—*Lā ilāha*, 'there is no deity'—it goes on to affirm the Truth—*illa'Llāh*, 'save God'—before Whom it locates man in a way which both invites him to reflection and defies analysis.

For some people, the *Shahāda* is a blazing proof. To others, it seems enigmatic and baffling. But whether one adheres to it following a lightning-flash of inspiration, or after a process of intellectual maturation, it is far more than a statement which invites one to take a particular mental course, for it engages the entire human being.

Announcing the absolute and hence exclusive reality of God, the *Shahāda* implies the inexorable necessity of conforming to Him, of submitting to His will, which is the exact meaning of the word *islām*. It is from this that the second formula, a logical and providential consequence of the first, derives all of its significance: *Muḥammadun rasūlu'Llāh*, 'Muhammad is the messenger of God': there is no better means of realising this conformity and this submission than by following the path mapped out by the Messenger.

To tread this path is, firstly, to accept the revealed Book, the Qur'an, and to put its injunctions into practice; and secondly, to conform to the teachings and the example of the man who was the vehicle of the Revelation: Muhammad. To be *muslim*, that is, to submit to the divine will, is in principle nothing more than this.

The confession of God's absolute reality and of one's freedom to submit to Him suffices to restore all meaning to a human life devalued by contemporary unbelief and confusion. But it does not demand an exorbitant price in return. Just as the basic confession of faith which is the *Shahāda* is remarkably simple and obvious, so also the other elements of Islamic faith and doctrine demand no arduous intellectual effort before they can be grasped and accepted. As for the practise of the religion, it may certainly appear demanding to those who are hostile to any form of discipline, but in fact it is easy and flexible enough to work with all circumstances of life, even in our age; and the duties which it lays down are not beyond the capacity of any human being possessed of a little goodwill. On the contrary, the effectiveness of their practice is amply demonstrated in the preservation of a sane equilibrium of soul and body.

It is none the less clear that this kind of religious observance, however easy it may be, still seems too constricting to many of our contemporaries, since the rejection of all kinds of discipline, encouraged by 'anti-authoritarian' theories of psychoanalysis and other modish 'philosophical' ideas, is such a specific feature of the modern mind. The prostration performed during the ritual prayer, which expresses the worshipper's longing to submit entirely to the Divine Sovereign, could not be more remote from the general movement of secularisation and 'liberation' which, according to a famous slogan, does not recognise 'any god or master' over man.

The practise of Islam is also a remembrance (*dhikr*) of God, Who, in the Qur'an (11:152), has announced: 'Remember Me, and I shall remember you'. Obviously this stands in direct conflict with the conventional modern lifestyle, which, lost in a senseless profusion of distractions, cares and anguishes, is in a systematic and general state of forgetfulness (*ghafla*) towards the Creator. Remembrance, which pervades the Muslim life, keeps man in communication with the centre of all things, whereas forgetfulness transforms him into a peripheral being subjugated by the external, quantitative aspect of the world and to the cosmic acceleration which is so clearly visible in these last years of the twentieth century.

The typically modern and secularised man stands at the precise antipodes of the *muslim* in surrender to the will of God. Unable to prostrate himself, incapable of worship, immersed in the flood of possibilities unleashed by a quantitative civilisation which offers him everything except the indispensable, and which neglects the one thing which gives meaning to life, he lives in a state of discontent for which he has found no effective cure, despite the number and unprecedented variety of the resources at his disposal. This impotence has served to aggravate his state of revolt against current conditions, and particularly against the final vestiges of the normative order derived from the religious traditions, and hence from God. It is thus that he has become the *homme révolté* so emblematic of our century.

Although Camus still ascribed some spiritual and moral values to this '*homme révolté*', these are now empty of any cautiousness which might flow from transcendence or religious faith; and do not take long to crumble and evaporate. One may affirm this regarding the 'counter-culture' which, pushing onward to the new age, tends to destroy everything which still resembles a social and moral order.

Of course, the 'counter-culture' can be justified inasmuch as it has rejected a quantitative civilisation which reduces man to the functions of producer and consumer, and which is therefore incapable of giving any satisfaction to his most profound and central aspirations. But in the great majority of cases, the counter-culture seeks to exploit legitimate reactions, particularly those of the young, and turn them to yet more tasks of subversion and destruction. It ends by creating a human being whose only variables are those governed by his functional and carnal instincts.

A man fallen into such nihilism could not be further removed from Islam. Since he has forgotten God, God has forgotten him.

For him, the human condition no longer has real sense. He is no longer a man, save in an accidental, fragmentory fashion.

There is a sense in which someone who has reached this extreme point of the modern process has set himself lower than the animals, since these latter are bound to the normalcy of their species and cannot transgress their own limits. This is why they always retain a certain innocence, unlike man, who possesses, as well as the possibility of raising himself above all creatures, the ability to lose himself and to fall to the lowest state of degradation.

At the opposite pole to this condition of revolt and subversion, the Muslim man is aware of having been created by God, Who has breathed His spirit into him and has charged him with being His witness and representative on this earth. Thus he is the most central of all creatures, since it is he who manifests the divine attributes most clearly. All creation lies subject to his command, but only by virtue of the authority which he holds from God, and to Whom he owes absolute submission.

Having made man into His representative, His lieutenant or His vicar (a translation sometimes used for the word *khalīfa*) on earth, God has charged him with a responsibility, or a 'trust' (*amāna*) which, among all creatures, it is his unique duty to discharge. On this subject the Qur'an articulates itself in terms which remain striking even in translation:

> *We offered the Trust unto the heavens, the earth, and the mountains, but they shrank from bearing it, and were afraid of it. And man assumed it; he who has proved a tyrant and a fool.* (Qur'an, XXXIII:72)

This trust is a formidable one, for it confers upon man the freedom to choose between good and evil, truth and falsehood, Heaven and hell. It invests the human condition with grandeur, but a grandeur which carries with it a terrible risk, in that man has shown himself to be 'a tyrant and a fool'. Islam gives him exactly the right methods of fending off this risk, and of using his liberty in works which lead, through his submission, to what is good, what is true, and to God.

Against the modern agnosticism which is unable to define man and the deeper reasons for his presence on earth, Islam opposes a perfectly coherent anthropology which replies to the most fundamental questions which may be posited. In this regard it is essential to remark that Islam appeals to man's intellect rather than to his sentimentality. By 'intellect' here, however, we mean that which is primordial, 'adamic', essential; not the capacity for involved reasoning. For Islam does not address itself solely to the sages and philosophers of this world, but rather to man as he is created, with his capacity to conceive of the Absolute and to choose freely that which conforms to it and leads towards it.

As the religion of Truth, Islam confers meaning on the human condition, which can be explained only as a function of the Absolute, and thereby abolishes the nihilistic absurdity of the modern world. It reconciles man to himself and to creation, bringing the most effective possible remedy to the sickness of our time.

This sickness is, in its way, the consequence of the revolt of Iblīs, the fallen angel, whom some spectacular passages of the Qur'an describe attempting to seize the incomparable privilege of the condition in which God has placed man, and then living out the drama of his error and his disgrace. According to this account, God, after creating Adam, commanded the angels to prostrate themselves before him. All the angels did so, with the exception of Iblīs, who explained his refusal by saying: *I am better than he; You created me from fire, and created him from clay.* When God expelled him, the devil implored, *Grant me a respite until the Day of Resurrection.*

Iblīs was granted this respite, and ever since that time has made use of it by deflecting men from the 'straight Path':

> *I shall come upon them from before them and from behind them and from their right and from their left . . .*
>
> *God said: 'Go forth from here, degraded, banished. I shall fill Gehenna with you all, and with those who shall follow you.'* (VII:11–18)

Even Adam was overwhelmed by the tempter. But he repented, and God accepted his repentance, and promised him and his wife that He would guide them: *And whoso follows My guidance shall neither go astray nor come to grief.* (XX:123)

This guidance is the 'perennial religion', which over the ages has assumed many expressions, and the final and definitive form of which is Islam, as incarnated in the revelation addressed to Muhammad. Like the earlier religions, Islam allows man to escape the curse which falls on those who follow Iblīs, and to fulfil the true vocation of man, which is to submit to the Creator, while enjoying the privileges and blessings promised the descendants of the primordial man:

> *We have honoured the children of Adam. We carry them on the land and the sea, and have made provision of good things for them, and have preferred them markedly above many of those whom We created.* (XVII:70)

Islam, therefore, does not deny man a full enjoyment of the blessings which God has accorded him, provided that they are acknowledged:

> *O you who believe! Eat of the good things which We have accorded you, and thank God, if it is He that you worship.* (II:172)

As the religion of equilibrium, it acknowledges this world as well as the next, although it is understood that the latter is to be preferred:

Do not neglect your share in the world. (XXVIII:77)
Truly, the Afterlife is better for you than this world. (XCIII:4)

Islam sets man on the way to an Afterlife which is preferable to anything which could be imagined in this world, but—as we shall see in the following chapters—it also offers him a method of using the better things of 'this world' by harmoniously organising the individual and the collective life. For it is the Will of God—and Islam is the submission to that Will—that people should be content.

There is a fact which is germane in this connection: the Arabic word *islām*, 'submission', is closely related to *silm*, or *salām*, meaning 'peace'. For submitting to God brings about peace, the precondition for happiness.

Here the objection might be voiced that the Muslims of today do not exactly present a picture of happiness and of peace. There are many ways of responding to this, but for now we shall confine ourselves to a few brief remarks, which may suffice until we return to the present situation of the Islamic world.

Firstly, it must be recognised that all religions in our time are in a state of crisis, Islam included—although probably to a lesser degree than the others. None of them, in any case, may fairly be judged if we take as our major criterion the condition of the people who supposedly profess it. The Muslims are in general aware that they live in a manner far removed from the true ideals of the Revelation vouchsafed to their prophet, and willingly acknowledge that if they were to follow its commandments their whole existence would be transformed. Islam has never been implemented completely at any time since its initial phase, the era of the Prophet and the first four 'rightly-guided' Caliphs; and the Muslim community, the *umma*, has always in consequence retained a certain nostalgia for that privileged age. Of course, over the centuries there have been periods of florescence, but no-one would seriously claim that we are living though such a time now. The evidence suggests, in fact, that the precise opposite is the case: the Muslim world, like everywhere else, is experiencing a state of crisis and decay unprecedented in its history.

None the less, one cannot deny that the malaise from which the world of Islam is suffering is quite different from the crisis of the industrialised West: its moral and spiritual foundations are not being challenged in the same way, and the great majority of people in the Muslim world retain their traditional faith. The crisis through which their countries are now passing is of a substantially more material order, since some, particularly those of Asia, are among the poorest to be found anywhere on the planet. This predicament, which can to some extent be attributed to the legacy of the erstwhile colonial powers, is certainly the cause of great misery; but it has not generally compromised the human dignity even of the most deprived. For Islam confers upon man a certain nobility which is unimpaired by poverty, and may sometimes even be enhanced by it. It cannot be denied that Islam, in the midst of the greatest destitution, preserves a sense of meaning in life, and protects that essential quality which makes life worth living.

In the light of this perspective, Islam, whether in the wealthy but demoralised West or in the material poverty of the so-called 'Third World', represents the clearest, most basic and most explicit response to the modern challenge. To those individuals and societies which accept it, and put it into practice, it offers the most precious and active remedy for the sickness of our time.

SOURCE TEXTS

The most perfect form

In the name of God, the Compassionate, the Merciful.
By the fig, and the olive,
By Mount Sinai,
And by this secure land.
We have created man in the most perfect form,
Then We reduced him to the lowest of the low,
Save those who believe, and do good works; theirs is a reward unfailing.
So who will say henceforth that you lie about the Judgement?
Is not God the most conclusive of all judges?

Qur'an, XCV: 'The Fig'

The meeting place

Islam is the meeting between God as such and man as such.

God as such: that is to say God envisaged, not as He manifested Himself in a particular way at a particular time, but independently of history and inasmuch as He is what He is and also as by His nature He creates and reveals.

Man as such: that is to say man envisaged, not as a fallen being needing a miracle to save him, but as man, a theomorphic being endowed with an intelligence capable of conceiving of the Absolute and with a will capable of choosing what leads to the Absolute.

Frithjof Schuon, *Understanding Islam*

Springboard of the Afterlife

As vicegerent of God, having received the management of the earth from Him, having, under God, the obligation to use his powers of reflection and of reason, the Muslim is not encouraged to hold the things of this world in contempt or to ignore them. On the contrary, he is required to establish the terrestrial City, in which he must make justice and peace reign, knowing full well that this City is nothing of itself, *for everything perishes, save the Face of God* (Qur'an, XXVIII:88). The life of this world is the springboard to the next, which shall follow the Last Hour, the Resurrection and Judgement, the only permanent thing, which shall bring a glorious reward to those who had done good, and terrible punishment for those who had disobeyed the Almighty. The goods of this world are not condemned; their usufruct is permitted to the faithful, who may use and enjoy them in accordance with the Divine Law and in their awareness of their own fragility. In using and enjoying them, but without allowing their hearts to fasten upon them, they thank God in poverty and in wealth, blessing Him in their triumphs and patiently tolerating their misfortunes, contemplating the testimonies of the Prophets and the supreme example which shall remain, until the end of centuries, the teaching and life of the Prophet of Islam.

Louis Gardet, *Les Hommes de l'Islam*

The secular slander

Judaism and Christianity make no secret of their inability to cope with the tide of materialism and invasion of the West by atheism. Both of them are completely taken off guard, and from one decade to the next one can surely see how seriously diminished their resistance is to this tide that threatens to sweep everything away. The materialist atheist sees in classical Christianity nothing more than a system constructed by men over the last two thousand years designed to ensure the authority of a minority over their fellow men. He is unable to find in Judaeo-Christian writings any language that is even vaguely similar to his own . . ..

When one mentions Islam to the materialist atheist, he smiles with a complacency that is only equal to his ignorance of the subject. In common with the majority of Western intellectuals, of whatever religious persuasion, he has an impressive collection of false notions about Islam.

One must, on this point, allow him one or two excuses. Firstly, apart from the newly-adopted attitudes prevailing among the highest Catholic authorities, Islam has always been subject in the West to a so-called 'secular slander.' Anyone in the West who has acquired a deep knowledge of Islam knows just to what extent its history, dogma and aims have been distorted. One must also take into account the fact that documents published in European languages on this subject (leaving aside highly specialised studies) do not make the work of a person willing to learn any easier.

Maurice Bucaille, *The Bible, the Quran and Science*

2

Man: axis of creation

FOR modern man, the universe has been reduced to one sole level of reality circumscribed by space and time. Creation is an accumulation of phenomena which only experimentation based on quantitative norms may validly apprehend. In consequence, the world appears as a more or less coherent, more or less absurd conglomeration of objects from which philosophical and scientific thought has progressively excluded any intervention on the part of higher principles, ultimately announcing that it is governed solely by chance. This is the thesis developed by an eminent Nobel laureate, Professor Jacques Monod—duly supported by learned proofs—in a famous book whose success clearly demonstrates the precision with which it gives expression to the modern frame of mind.

A similar conception of the universe dictates man's attitude to nature, which the moderns regard as an object which they may dispose of as they please in order to satisfy either their needs, their ambitions or their caprices. Since they fail to discern any deep significance in it, or anything which merits respect—it is, after all, the product of chance—and having thereby desacralised it, they go on to exploit and violate it, destroying its harmony and eventually provoking the ecological crisis which is causing such justifiably deep disquiet to world opinion.

By contrast, the Muslim sees in creation the work of God, the manifestation of His signs and glory. For him, the cosmos, and all that it contains, is an array of symbols which speak of a higher order of reality. In nature there is nothing absurd or fortuitous;

everything is endowed with a significance which may be discerned by anyone who remains unblinded by the mentality and biases of modernity.

This discernment, which is also the capacity for respect and wonderment at the Creator's works, allows one to see in all things a testimony to the divine unity and omnipotence. For *all creatures in heaven and earth submit to God, willingly or unwillingly, and unto Him shall they be returned* (III:83).

Because nothing lies outside the scope of this divine omnipotence, there is nothing in creation which is not submitted to God, and therefore *muslim*. And yet, among created beings, only man can be such in a fully conscious way. To be truly Muslim is not merely to submit to this submission, it is actively to take it upon oneself through a choice which represents the cardinal act of all human life: the 'yes' to God, to His truth and His unity which, in one way or another, is disclosed by all created things.

Man has been blessed with privileges which distinguish him absolutely from other creatures. God, Who *breathed into him of His spirit* (XXXII:9), has granted him intelligence. It is therefore with the knowledge of why he acts that he makes his choice. For *have We not shown him the two ways?* (XC:10) God also says in the Qur'an: *We have shown him the way, whether he be grateful or disbelieving* (LXXVI:3).

The centrality of man's station on earth means that if his choice is not that of submission and conformity to the divine will, if he follows the way of disbelief and revolt, then he must become a source of disorder in creation. Present conditions demonstrate this exactly. Modern civilisation, which constitutes a rebellion against the divine order, is destroying the equilibrium of nature, and has raised the spectre of cataclysms which may obliterate all life on the planet.

The 'Greens', who hope to rescue nature from the danger of such destruction, would unquestionably be more effective if they strove at the same time to restore order within themselves. For by virtue of the correspondance which exists between macrocosm and microcosm, man cannot exercise any truly benign action in the world without setting himself in accord with the divine Source of all goodness, and accepting it as his inspiration.

In the Qur'an, God says: *We shall show them Our signs on the horizons and within themselves until it becomes clear to them that it is the Truth* (XLI:53). This implies that contemplation of the external creation is also a means of penetrating into the interior world which corresponds to it. Many other Qur'anic passages insist on the transparency of nature, and on the signs which it holds for *those who have intelligence*, and who *meditate on the creation of the heavens and the earth*. To these people, the sacred text states, as though to refute in advance the modern hypotheses regarding the supposed 'randomness' of creation: *Our Lord! You have not created this in vain! You are Sublime!* (III:191)

By virtue of the intellect which has been conferred upon him, man is able not only to contemplate the divine order present in the universe, but also to intervene positively and to live in harmony with it. But if he does not wish to see the signs of God therein, if he denies His sovereignty, and believes himself able to do as he wishes with all things in this world, then he desacralizes nature, subverts the equilibrium, and ultimately becomes the most malignant element in creation.

Man's choice therefore engages his total responsibility, in keeping with the central position which is his in creation. Of course, *no man shall bear the burden of another* (LIII:38), but groups, communities and nations also possess their own responsibilities. For *God changes nothing for a people until they change what is in themselves* (XIII:11).

This responsibility implies that man, as an individual just as much as a member of a group of which he is a part, must give an account of all the actions which he performed during his life on earth. One of the expressions which in Islam designate the Last Judgement is the 'Day of Reckoning'.

This is a notion to which the modern and profane mind is especially resistant, since the concept of a judgement implies an inevitable limitation of the total power which man claims to exercise over the world. Nevertheless, if one is honest one must acknowledge that it does conform to the innate sense of justice which each one of us carries in the depths of his soul. Can one really admit that all the evil which is endlessly visible in this world, that all the acts of wickedness and horror which are so routinely committed and which are so abhorrent to the conscience, shall never be judged by a higher authority? Is it conceivable that those responsible for suffering, for oppression and for disorder will never be punished? Even though some 'philosophers' believe that they can reply with a cynical affirmative to such questions, it seems evident that the people of our age have not entirely lost the profound feeling, however confused it may be, that there does exist an ultimate and supreme justice which must some day make itself apparent. In any case, this is for Islam an absolute certainty, and the Qur'an repeatedly declares the Day of Judgement to be 'inexorable': *There is no doubt concerning that Day; God fails not His promise* (III:9).

Man carries a responsibility which is fuller still, since Islam does not recognise the idea of original sin. He has been created *in the most perfect form* (XCV:4), and it is for this reason that if he fails to follow the road to which God summons him he falls lower than all other creatures. According to the Prophet Muhammad, everyone is born pure, and commits no sins until he has reached maturity. Another of his sayings is often cited in the same regard: 'Every child is born with the primordial natural disposition (*fiṭra*), and only his parents make of him a Jew, a Christian or a Zoroastrian.'

This concept of the *fiṭra*, or the 'human norm', which in a way resembles that of the 'conscience', means that simply by being born into the human state man possesses an innate knowledge of truth and goodness. This knowledge, attenuated for most people, must be actualised through the light of revelation and the practice of Islam according to the example set by the Prophet, which is the *fiṭra*, the perfect norm, for all humanity.

The disbeliever, by contrast, is veiled by his deliberate denial from this inner light which is the *fiṭra*, through which he would be perfectly capable of understanding the truths made manifest by revelation. Thus he cannot excuse himself by claiming ignorance; in fact his responsibility is thereby made still more acute.

A Qur'anic passage outlines this idea:

> *When your Lord brought forth from the descendants of Adam, from their reins, their seed, He made them testify against themselves, saying:*
> *'Am I not your Lord?'*
> *'Yes,' they said, 'We bear witness!'*
> *That was lest you should say at the Day of Resurrection: 'Of this we were unaware.'* (VII:172)

According to the traditional commentaries, this means that God has made with all men, before their birth, a compact of faith whose seal they carry in their hearts. Every man is therefore born with a predisposition to receive Islam. But he also possesses the fatal freedom to break the compact, and, in place of returning to the Unity which lies at the centre of all things and of his own self, to go out to lose himself hopelessly in the peripheral illusions of multiplicity.

Westerners, apt to attribute an alleged fatalism to Islam, often believe that it does not possess a true concept of free will. On the contrary, however, it attaches a fundamental importance to it, since without it man would have no true choice between submitting to God and rebellion, and, by extension, could not be held responsible for his acts. Without freedom, Islam could be no more than a passive and inert surrender equivalent to that of the inanimate and animal creatures, rather than the conscious and fully accepted obedience which it must be for human beings.

Nevertheless, one could object that because of predestination—which Islam does teach—God has fixed in advance the destiny of all men, and that there is therefore no true freedom, and that man cannot be taken to task for his conduct. It is true that the Qur'an makes a number of references to the 'divine Decree' (*qadar*) according to which all things have been created and determined. It is for this reason that—for man—*God has created and fixed his destiny, and has then made easy his path* (LXXX:19–20). It is also written that: *No disaster befalls in the earth or in yourselves but that it was in a Book before We brought it into being* (LVII:22).

One may note first of all that the doctrine of predestination is not unique to Islam, but flows inevitably from the idea of divine omnipotence. The Bible makes numerous references to it, which have none the less not induced Jewish and Christian thinkers to challenge the principle of human liberty. A Christian philosopher such as Leibnitz was able to draw the following conclusion: 'Without doubt, all is determined, but since we do not know what has been decided and resolved, or how, we must discharge our duty according to the intellect which we are vouchsafed by God, and in compliance with the rules which He has laid down for us.'

In Islam the seeming contradiction between human freedom and the predestination of our acts has been the subject of extensive theological disputes, which refer very frequently to the following passage of the Qur'an: *Whoever wills, may choose a path to his Lord; but you do not will, unless God wills* (LXXVI:29–30). In general, Muslim thought sees the solution of the problem as lying in the acceptance of the divine volition which corresponds to the fundamental concept of Islam. But it has equally been remarked that the contradiction is resolved if one defines human liberty as a limited participation in the absolute and infinite liberty of God. In any event, the ability to choose freely between conformity to or rejection of the divine will is an experience which no-one could reasonably deny.

Whatever the case may be, if man is possessed of some sort of freedom, it might at first glance appear that he renounces it in making the act of submission. This would obviously be so were it a matter of submitting to something which was itself created and subject to the limitations of terrestrial existence. But it is a different matter altogether to submit to God, Who is absolutely free and unrestricted by constraints or limitations of any kind.

The freedom of choice enjoyed by man, which is a participation in the unlimited freedom of God, is expressed in the central position which he occupies in creation. By making him His 'vicegerent', or representative, on earth, God has given him, along with something of His own liberty, the possiblity of using it well or badly.

This possibility is symbolised in the Qur'an, as it is in the Bible, in terms of the forbidding of the fruit of the 'tree of eternal life' to the first human couple:

> *O Adam! Dwell in the Garden, you and your wife. Eat of its fruits where you will; but do not approach this tree, lest you be among the wrongdoers.*
>
> (VII:19)

Of course, in disregarding the divine prohibition the first man was making use of the freedom granted him by his Creator, but at the same time he circumscribed it, his disobedience making him more dependent on the limitations of existence, so that he was more narrowly subject to the material world and the trials of his earthly estate:

> *And God said: Go down! Ye shall be enemies one to another. There will be for you on earth a habitation, and provision for a while.*
>
> (VII:24)

Nevertheless, Adam repented, *receiving words from his Lord; and He relented towards him.* (II:37) God accepted his repentance, and then gave him 'guidance':

> *Whoever follows My guidance, no fear shall come upon him, neither shall he grieve.* (VII:123)

Thus, according to the Islamic perspective, Adam became despite his sin the first prophet in the long line of bearers of the universal revelation, of which the last was Muhammad, and which included all the messengers, known or unknown, through whom human beings have received guidance. Having returned to God, Who appointed him prophet, Adam did not transmit the curse of his sin to his descendants; on the contrary he bequeathed the promise of a divine grace which shall embrace all those who return to the *fiṭra* and follow the way mapped out by the Messengers.

The symbolic example of Adam remains perfectly valid today, since, despite his fall, man retains his central position in the cosmos together with the privileges which flow from it. This position can always be made fully effective, since the human condition permits of a close intimacy with God even if we are not aware of it:

> *We have created man, and We know what his soul whispers to him, and We are closer to him than his jugular vein.* (L:16)

The return to God through an act of penitence analogous to that of Adam is the best use to which man may put the freedom with which he has been endowed. It signifies a restoration of the human condition to a state of harmony with the Creator's intention.

To the modern mind, the Muslim who submits to the divine order and binds himself to a series of religious obligations and rules of life may appear less free than a wholly secularised man who lives in accordance with his inclinations and instincts. Yet in reality the Muslim discipline is no deprivation of freedom, but a simple re-establishment, in the individual and collective life, of an order of values and a rhythm which accord with the total nature of man and with his deepest aspirations, as well as with the harmony of the cosmos.

There is no question but that freedom as it is understood in our day is a precious commodity, the value of which is especially evident to those who have been deprived of it. But it always remains a very relative thing, and is never realised perfectly on this earthly plane. Any man who enjoys it in some limited way and aspires to possess it more fully is finally driven to admit that it eludes him to the extent that he pursues it. The revolutions which have made so many promises in this regard have certainly suppressed some restrictions, but only by the device of introducing others. And how many crimes have not been committed, how many tyrannies have not arisen, in the name of freedom!

Islam, for its part, is at once more realistic and more idealistic. Aware that men in this inferior world are possessed of no more than a limited degree of liberty, it teaches them in the first place to make proper use of it, since it knows their frailty well. It is in this, in the final analysis, that all of the Muslim life consists. The accomplishment of each religious rite is in its way a renewal of the free and fundamental choice that the believer has made for the divine unity and reality in preference to the multiplicity and illusions of the world. Thus equipped with practical means of conforming day by day to God's will, the Muslim participates ever more fully in his total liberation.

In this way Islam offers man the possibility of returning to God following the example of Adam, of receiving guidance, and of filling the central place in creation which is his real destiny. He no longer regards this creation with the perverse eye of the moderns, for whom the universe and nature, reduced to quantitative laws, are no more than random and meaningless events; instead he contemplates the 'signs' of the divine reality.

It is only thus that man is able to reinstate his original sacred function as God's vicegerent on earth. No longer will he be a miscreant who threatens nature with destruction, but rather a guardian and protector who assumes full responsibility towards the created order.

It is important to state, too, that since human freedom, which Islam teaches man to use correctly, is, in the Muslim perspective, to be equated more than anything else with a condition of readiness to accomplish the divine will and to practise one's religion without hindrances, then each time that obstacles or restrictions stand in the way of this freedom to worship God in a way conforming to His commandments, Muslims consider it their duty to struggle for its full reinstatement.

This struggle is one form of *jihād*, the 'holy war', as this Arabic term is most often translated, without beginning to suggest its real meaning, which expresses something nearer to the idea of 'collective effort'. Such is the true significance of the struggle led by Muslims against the colonial regimes, and against every form of domination and subjugation which is hostile to the spirit and practice of Islam. Such liberation struggles have made many martyrs over the centuries, and continue to do so today.

In accordance with the authentic Islamic spirit, however, such combatants must always recall that in God's sight freedom is a means and not an end in itself. This is why, whatever form the struggle may take, the battle cry of the true *mujāhidīn*, the warriors of *jihād*, has always been, and continues to be, *Allāhu akbar*—'God is greater still.'

SOURCE TEXTS

The human norm (*fiṭra*)

Set your purpose for religion as a man by nature upright—the nature (given) by God in which He has created man. There is no altering God's creating. That is the right religion, yet most people do not know.

Qur'an, XXX:30

Light upon light

God is the Light of the heavens and the earth. The allegory of His light is as a niche wherein is a lamp. The lamp is in a glass. The glass is as it were a shining star. Kindled it is, from a blessed tree, an olive neither of the East nor of the West, whose oil would almost glow forth though no fire touched it. Light upon light! God guides to His light whom He will, and He speaks to mankind in allegories, and He is Knower of all things.

Qur'an, XXIV:35

In the heart of the Muslim

The 'allegory of His light' signifies: 'the allegory of His light in the heart of the Muslim'. This is a reference to the light which God sets in the heart of His servants, in the form of knowledge and love of God, belief in Him and remembrance of Him. It is also His light which He sends unto men, when He gives them life by implanting it in their hearts.

The heart of man is illuminated. It is close to knowing truth by its own nature (*fiṭra*) and intelligence, and is followed up by the Revelation which exercises its own action so that the light of his *fiṭra* which he is given by God becomes still more luminous. The light of the *fiṭra* combined with the light of the Revelation allows this truth to be expressed as 'light upon light'.

Ibn al-Qayyim, *Tafsīr* (Qur'anic commentary)

Predestination

We have created all things in accordance with a decree.

LIV:49

Say: Nothing shall come to us save that which God has written for us.

IX:51

He has created everything, and has meted out for it a measure determined.

XXV:2

God brings His command to pass.
God has set a measure determined for all things.

LXV:3

We have determined; excellent are We as determiners!

LXXVII:23

Ḥadīth

And God spoke to Adam, saying: 'This group have I created for Paradise, and the acts of its members shall conform to the acts of the People of Paradise'. And He said also: 'This group have I created for hellfire, and the acts of its members shall conform to the acts of the people of hellfire'. Having heard this teaching from the Prophet, a man asked, 'To what purpose, then, do we act in one wise or another?'—and he replied: 'When God creates a man who is destined for Paradise, the acts of such a man will render him worthy thereof, until he dies and enters therein. And when He creates someone who is destined for hell, his acts shall resemble the acts of the people of hell, and when he dies, he shall enter therein.'

The Messenger of God also said to his Companions:

'There is not one amongst you whose place has not been predestined by God, whether it be in Heaven or in hell.'

The Companions said: 'O Messenger of God! Since God has decided our places in advance, can we rely on this certitude and renounce our religious and moral duties?'

'No indeed,' he replied, 'since the just shall accomplish good works, and obey God, while the evil shall commit sins.'

Cited by Ahmad Galwash, *The Religion of Islam*

By what right does man exploit the animal kingdom?

One of the longest epistles of the Ikhwān al-Ṣafā' is devoted to animals. In this important treatise, the Ikhwān [. . .] devote a long section, exceptional in length alone within all the epistles, to 'the dispute between man and the animals'. This beautifully written story, which is extremely timely reading today in the light of the ecological crisis, discusses the reasons given by man for his right to dominate and destroy the animal kingdom, and the response of the animals, which nullifies all the arguments of man based on his purely human advantages such as the power of ratiocination or invention. Only when animals see that among men there are saints, who in returning to God also fulfil the deepest purpose of the animal kingdom, do they agree to obey man and to serve him. The moral of the story is that man has the right to dominate animals only on condition that he remain conscious of his vice-gerency (*khilāfa*), of his being God's representative on earth and from another point of view the representative of all earthly creatures before God. Otherwise, he has no cogent reason whatsoever to rule and dominate other creatures, and in fact will pay dearly for usurping a function to which he is not entitled save as the child of that Adam who, as the Holy Quran asserts, was taught the 'names' of all things.

Seyyed Hossein Nasr, *Islamic Science*

3

The eternal message and its final bearer

We have sent you with the truth, as a bearer of glad tidings and a warner; and there is no nation amongst whom a warner has not passed. (XXXV:24)

We reveal to you as We revealed to Noah and the prophets after him, and as We inspired Abraham and Ishmael and Isaac and Jacob and the tribes, and Jesus, Job and Jonah, Aaron and Solomon, and as We imparted the Psalms unto David.

Messengers We have mentioned unto you before, and messengers We have not mentioned to you. And God spoke unto Moses directly. (IV:163–64)

THUS, by the revealed word of the Qur'an, is the mission of Muhammad, the Prophet of Islam, situated within the framework of the universal revelation. He came to remind men, always inclined to forget or distort it, of the eternal message of the divine Truth which had not changed since the Creation—for that which changes cannot be Truth—a message which God had from time to time reaffirmed in a way which permitted all people in every age and nation, without exception, to know of it.

But with Muhammad, the *Seal of the Prophets* (XXXIII:40), the cycle of Revelation came to an end. And sure enough, no major religion has been founded since his death, and no personality comparable to his has appeared in the annals of mankind.

The forms in which the revelation was cast have varied greatly since Noah, even since Adam, but certain elements remain consistent in all the authentic traditions which go back to a non-human source, or—in other words—to the sacred. The prime element among these is of a metaphysical order: the affirmation of a transcendent Reality which is exclusive and which wields absolute power. Specifically, it is nothing other than the *Shahāda* of Islam: *Lā ilāha illa'Llāh*, 'there is no deity save God', which in a formula worthy of the divine perfection sums up the fundamental truth which, while already familiar to the wisdom of antiquity and the earlier revelations, had never been expressed with the same density.

A second element to be found in all revelations is the notion that men are responsible for their acts, and that they shall be brought to judgement when this earthly existence comes to its close. In the previous chapter we saw how Islam lays especial emphasis on this point.

Since God is eminently 'compassionate and merciful'—according to a formula which recurs constantly in the Qur'an—and since 'His mercy outstrips His wrath', it would have been inconceivable for Him to have left, for thousands of years, the greater part of the earth's inhabitants in ignorance and misguidance. The Qur'an therefore makes the specific announcement that a 'warner' came to every one of these peoples, and, addressing itself to Muhammad, gives him clearly to understand that revelation is not be conceived as being limited to the prophets who are mentioned by name in the Book.

In this respect it is interesting to note that according to much recent research in the fields of ethnology and archeology, even the most 'backward' and isolated peoples have always believed—with a greater or lesser degree of confusion—in a supreme divine power. Certain tribes of the Pacific basin, Africa and South America, far removed from what we call 'civilisation', often retain the vestiges of a highly sophisticated metaphysical knowledge the origin of which has not been well explained. There can be no doubt that each received, in a remote past, the teachings of a 'warner', whose message, as the centuries passed, became obscured and amended until only superstitions remained, these being often of the most crude variety.

Such was the case with the Arabs of the *jāhiliyya*, the 'Age of Ignorance' which preceded the revelation of Islam. Mecca, a merchant city built around the Kaᶜba temple constructed in an earlier age by Abraham (*Ibrāhīm*) and his son Ishmael in honour of the One God, *Allāh*, had by now become the centre of a grossly polytheistic and often malevolent cult.

The man who was destined to transmit the final revelation of the prophetic cycle was born in about 570 of the Christian era, in a town which, surrounded by inhospitable deserts, had for centuries been cut off from the great religious and civilising currents of the outside world. He belonged to the ruling tribe of Quraysh; orphaned at an early age he was brought up by an uncle already burdened with a large family, and came to make a living as a caravan agent, a vocation which afforded him numerous opportunities to make long voyages, most particularly to Syria.

Already known to all who dealt with him for his irreproachable virtue and sharp intelligence, he entered into the service of a widow belonging to his own aristocratic class: Khadīja, who stood at the head of an important trading house. It was not long before he married her; he was twenty-five, and she forty. He proved deeply attached to her, and never married again before her death.

Although Muhammad continued his commercial activity, he also began to make regular retreats in the desert for the purpose of meditation. Often, too, he performed the ritual circuits of the

Kaᶜba, a practice which had been perpetuated in an ancient tradition. His great piety addressed itself solely to *Allāh*, the supreme deity, and he turned away with distaste from the idols which stood in the sanctuary.

Then, at the age of forty, when he was in the cave of Ḥīra near Mecca, he beheld advancing towards him a being who radiated an almost blinding light. This was the Archangel Gabriel (*Jibrīl*), come to announce that God, *Allāh*, had chosen him to be His messenger (*rasūl*) to mankind. Seized with panic, he asked himself whether he had lost his reason, or had come under an attack from demonic forces. He found comfort and sustenance in Khadīja, who did not doubt for a moment the divine origin of the message, and the reality of the mission which had been entrusted to him.

After some time, the angel reappeared more and more frequently, confirming to Muhammad that he was indeed a Prophet of God, and dictating to him the first *sūras* of the Book, the remainder of which were to come over the following twenty-three years. In obedience to the divine command, the new apostle set to preaching the message among his Meccan compatriots, addressing the humble just as earnestly as he addressed the powerful.

The first *sūras* revealed at Mecca stress two dominant themes: recognition of the One God, Absolute, Infinite, All-powerful and without partners; and certainty in the inexorable conclusion, the final 'Hour', when men, having been judged for their works, shall be sent to hellfire or to eternal bliss. Inspired by these two fundamental truths, the Prophet's preaching called his compatriots to submit to the Almighty Creator of heaven and earth, Source of all goodness; but it also, necessarily, made a frontal attack on the official idolatry of the Meccans, and could scarcely have avoided provoking them into hostility.

None the less it also brought about some total and enthusiastic conversions. After Khadīja (the first woman Muslim), a small number of believers began to gather around Muhammad, which included his cousin ʿAlī, Zayd the freedman, Abū Bakr, a comfortably-off businessman, and several other men and women, mostly of humble standing. Faced with the nascent community of Islam, opposition, restricted at first to scornful words and gibes, became more virulent and intense, soon turning into an open persecution which threatened the lives of the Muslims and their leader, who were forced to endure every kind of outrage. Muslim blood flowed, and the new religion acquired its first martyrs.

The number of Muslims nevertheless continued to expand. Often it was the simple recitation of the Qur'an which brought about a conversion, for it surpassed in beauty and power anything which Arab poetry had been capable of expressing. Hearing the sacred text drew forth vibrant internal resonances which struck at the deepest level of a man's being, and often triggered a sudden response which brought him to conviction. The recitation of the Qur'an won converts even among some of Islam's most bitter enemies. One of these—though there were many others—was ʿUmar, a man of rare determination who, having at first decided to kill the Prophet, became one of his most intrepid companions.

Instead of subsiding, however, the persecution grew so ferocious that to avoid the needless loss of precious lives Muhammad sent a group of his supporters to seek refuge in Abyssinia. The Christian ruler of that country welcomed them warmly, and a tradition tells us that he was moved to tears by hearing that these Arabs had received a new revelation which accorded the most profound veneration to Jesus and the Blessed Virgin.

When some time had passed, many of these refugees returned to Mecca where, they believed, the persecution had abated. In fact, however, they found that they were no more secure, and were soon forced to prepare for a new exile.

During this first, Meccan, period of revelation there took place an event of the greatest importance in Muslim history: the

Night Journey, or *Miʿrāj*, which is mentioned in the following terms in the Qur'an:

> *Glory be to Him Who carried His servant by night from the Sacred Mosque to the Farthest Mosque, the neighbourhood whereof We have blessed, to show him certain of Our signs.* (XVII:1)

During this mystical experience the Prophet was first transported from the 'Sacred Mosque'—the Kaʿba of Mecca—to the 'Farthest Mosque', in Arabic *al-Masjid al-Aqṣā*, a name for the site of the Temple of Jerusalem. Then, from the sacred rock of the ancient sanctuary, he was raised up to the Seventh Heaven, meeting during his ascension the messengers whom God had sent to earth before him, most notably Abraham (*Ibrāhīm*), Moses (*Mūsā*) and Jesus (*ʿĪsā*). He performed the ritual prayer as imam for all the Prophets, and then found himself alone in the presence of God. For the founder of Islam, this was the confirmation that his mission truly stood in the line of the great monotheistic revelations, of which it constituted both synthesis and conclusion.

The following day, in Mecca, he described this miracle to his companions, and, while some were doubtful, Abū Bakr declared: 'I bear witness that Muhammad is truthful in every word he speaks!' From that day on, all Muslims have believed in the reality of the *Miʿrāj*; hence their abiding attachment to Jerusalem, which, after Mecca and Medina, is the third city of Islam.

At this period the early Muslims oriented themselves, when performing the ritual prayer, towards Jerusalem, which therefore constituted their *qibla*. It was only later, at Medina, that a Qur'anic revelation was received by the Prophet which instructed him that he should henceforth turn towards the Kaʿba of Mecca. This has been the *qibla* for Muslims ever since; although, according to certain traditions, the first *qibla* of Jerusalem must be reinstated towards the end of time, when the final Hour looms large.

Meanwhile, the hostility of Quraysh made the position of the first Muslim community at Mecca increasingly untenable. Tribal solidarity, thanks to which Muhammad had been able to count on a certain degree of protection on the part of his kinsmen, did not offer him a sufficient guarantee. It seemed fairly clear that Islam could make no further progress in the Meccan environment. On the other hand, a good number of outsiders travelling through the merchant city had heard the preaching of the Prophet and had been deeply impressed by it.

This was particularly the case with those who came from Yathrib, an oasis several days' voyage to the north of Mecca, and a number of whose inhabitants had already declared themselves as Muslims. Recognising in Muhammad an unsurpassable authority, they realised that no-one could better resolve the conflicts which were dividing their community. They therefore invited him and his companions to live at Yathrib, which soon came to be known as *Madīnat al-Nabī*: the City of the Prophet, or Medina.

Following a divine revelation, it was decided that the entire Muslim population would leave Mecca to seek refuge in the northern city. They set out in small groups to avoid attracting the attention of the Qurayshites. Before long no-one remained in the city except the Prophet, Abū Bakr and ʿAlī, together with a few of their closest relations and a small number of slaves.

The enemies of Islam understood well the danger which the departure of the Prophet would pose to them, and they resolved to take his life. When they tried to put their plan into execution, however, the Prophet managed to leave the town secretly in the company of Abū Bakr.

An armed contingent of Meccans was immediately sent out in pursuit of the fugitives, who, without divine protection, would certainly have been captured. It was some ten days (and numerous incidents later) before they arrived safely. On entering the oasis they were acclaimed by a great throng of Medinans who had come forth to welcome them. The emigration, in Arabic *hijra*, from which the word 'hegira' is derived, was complete. This immensely significant event, which took place in the year 622 of the Christian era, forms Year One of the Muslim calendar.

It would have been possible to inaugurate the Muslim calendar with, for instance, the birth of the Prophet, or with the first revelation received by him from Heaven. The Hegira was preferred over these alternatives because it marked the establishment of the City of God on earth.

From the time the Prophet arrived at Medina, the whole existence both of society and individuals organised itself in conformity with the commandments of God and His Messenger. The *Dār al-Islām*, the Islamic state installed at Medina, became the model destined to inspire Muslims for the centuries to come.

For Muslim piety, the Hegira is endowed with a further significance. Following the example of the emigrants, or *muhājirūn*, who had abandoned their homes and possessions at Mecca in order to serve God and follow the Prophet, the believers had to be prepared, in their love of God and fidelity to Islam, to detach themselves from what was precious to them of this world. For the mystics this theme has become that of the total submission to the divine will, and of the renunciation of self.

A substantial task presented itself immediately after the Hegira: organising the life of the new community, and laying the foundations of the state. At the time, the population of Medina was made up of a whole spectrum of groupings. Firstly, there were the *muhājirūn*, the emigrants who had fled the persecutions at Mecca. Then there were the local converts, the *anṣār* ('Helpers'), the number of whom was growing constantly. The Prophet established ties of brotherhood between these two groups, and inculcated a sense of solidarity which has never completely vanished from Muslim society.

Numerous Jews also lived at Medina. The Prophet did everything in his power to gain their confidence and goodwill, respecting their religion and their particular circumstances. Tradition has preserved the text of a directive which sets forth the attitude to be observed towards them: 'All Jews who choose to support our cause shall benefit from all the privileges enjoyed by the Muslims. They shall not be oppressed, neither shall there be any agitation against them. The Jews of Banū ᶜAwf (one of the Jewish tribes of the city) form a community with the believers. Between them goodwill and justice must prevail.'*

In this way, principles were laid down to govern relations between Muslims and adherents of other faiths, particularly Jews and Christians, who were the followers of divine messages explicitly recognised by Islam. This inaugurated a fundamental attitude of tolerance which, in general, and despite various crises for which the Muslims have not always been responsible, has been observed down the centuries, and continues to be maintained today.

The Jews of Medina, for their part, did not grasp the hand which was extended to them. With a few exceptions, they responded with a malign opposition, and finally with treason. Their presence became an obstacle to the consolidation of the Islamic state, and it became necessary to exile them.

Conflict between Mecca and the new Islamic state which was growing ever stronger and more developed, was inevitable, and two years after the Hegira open hostilities were begun. The principal event of this war was the Battle of Badr, in which the Muslims defeated a better-armed enemy three times their number. On this occasion the Prophet showed himself both an excellent strategist and a humanitarian leader: in contrast to the crude prevailing mores of the age, he obliged his troops to respect all captives, wounded fighters and non-combatants. A Qur'anic revelation came down which reminded the army of believers that they did not owe their victory to their own merit, but rather to the grace of God.

*It should be stated in passing that the other Jewish tribes were accorded the same rights given the ᶜAwf.

Bent on revenge, the Meccans soon prepared a new offensive against the Muslim state. Thirteen months after Badr, their army, considerably reinforced and including a powerful contingent of cavalry, marched on Medina. The Muslims, who were far less numerous, came out to meet them, and the two armies finally clashed on the plain of Uḥud. The Prophet's orders were badly implemented, or simply ignored, and his troops, after an initial success, suffered a reverse. Muhammad himself was wounded, and his enemies cried out that he was dead, which caused such panic among the Muslim defenders that only those who knew that he still lived continued the fight.

The Qurayshites, however, failed to exploit their success, although they did not give up their intention of putting paid to Islam and the threat which it posed to them once and for all. They arranged a third campaign, the main incident in which was the Battle of the Trench (*Khandaq*).

With two thousand men, the Meccan army represented a formidable force for the Arabia of the day. Since the Muslims could only muster a quarter of this number to oppose them, the Prophet chose to dig a trench sufficiently wide and deep to frustrate the enemy charges. Faced with this unexpected obstacle, the Qurayshites and their allies, whose supplies were running low, decided to terminate operations and to return home.

In spite of this major defensive success the security of Medina was still not conclusively established, since a serious menace was presenting itself from another direction. Khaybar, a prosperous oasis about 150 kilometres away, was inhabited by Jews who were allied with the Meccans against Islam. Before turning his attention to this hostile power, however, the Prophet wished to carry out something which was both an act of piety and a gesture of peace towards his old country: to the surprise of his Companions, he decided to embark upon a pilgrimage to Mecca.

Choosing the period of 'God's Truce', which the Qurayshites still respected as the occasion of the great sacred rite dating from the time of Abraham, he set out peacefully, surrounded by an unarmed group of the faithful. They halted at Ḥudaybiyya, at the boundaries of the sacred territory, but were unable to penetrate the city since the rulers refused them access.

In this place there occurred an episode whose symbolic significance is particularly emphasised by the mystical tradition within Islam: sitting beneath a tree, the Prophet received from each of his companions a renewal of their pledge of fidelity and readiness to lay down their lives.

A Meccan delegation came out to negotiate with Muhammad, and a truce was signed, according to the terms of which the Muslims agreed not to visit the Kaʿba for the time being, in exchange for a promise that they would be able to accomplish the pilgrimage rites the following year. At the same time, the two sides agreed to a cessation of hostilities for ten years.

Many of his companions were unhappy with this pact, which seemed to them humiliating and unfair, but the Prophet saw the benefit which it would bring to the Islamic cause. In the first place, the Muslims now had their hands free to act against Khaybar, which was subjecting Medina to a kind of economic blockade. The oasis was quickly occupied, despite the formidable fortresses which defended it. Towards the defeated parties the Prophet once more showed a clemency and mildness which contrasted radically with the practices usual at that time.

Islam made progress also in the interior of the Arabian peninsula, and a growing number of bedouins came to Medina to declare their loyalty to the Prophet. The Meccans began to feel more and more isolated; moreover, a good number of them, including some members of the ruling families, had already left the city and defected to the Muslim camp. Thus their principal chieftain, Abū Sufyān, came to realise that it would be better to submit without a fight.

In Year Eight of the Hegira, the army of believers was thus able to make its entrance into Mecca. Apart from one skirmish which left fifteen dead, the city fell almost without resistance. All those who had persecuted the Prophet and the Muslims feared reprisals, but there were none. Muhammad forgave all his enemies, and showed them a generosity which won them over definitively to the faith.

Surrounded by his Companions, the Prophet then returned to Medina where he continued to develop the organisation of the Muslim state. He received delegations from the most diverse regions of Arabia and even Syria, which came to announce the conversion of their people to Islam and their entry into his alliance.

The Muslim community, the *umma*, which had numbered no more than a few hundred believers when Muhammad, the refugee from Mecca, had established its foundations at Medina, had in ten years been transformed into an extensive and solidly organised state which the great powers of the day now had to reckon with. The Prophet had already sent letters to the rulers of the major states which bordered on Arabia, in particular to the emperors of Persia and Byzantium, to the Coptic patriarch of Egypt and the Negus of Abyssinia, urging them to embrace Islam. The Persian monarch disdainfully tore the letter to shreds, and Muhammad, when the news reached him, only said: 'May God tear his kingdom to shreds!' Precisely this happened a few years on, when the Muslim armies, in a crushing campaign, steamrollered this great power and overran the entire territory of Iran.

If, for his part, the Byzantine emperor Heraclius reacted with a little more sympathy, the same was not the case with his vassal, the prince of the Ghassanids to the north of the Muslim territory, who, upon receiving a similar letter, ordered the ambassador who had brought it to be murdered. This resulted in a war which, after the death of the Prophet, resulted in the conquest by Islamic forces of all the Syrian provinces of Byzantium.

In this tenth year of the Hegira the Prophet made known his intention to take part in the *Ḥajj*, the pilgrimage to Mecca. The announcement drew a vast response, and it was in the presence of 140,000 of the faithful that he accomplished the 'Farewell Pilgrimage' which marked the consummation of his earthly mission.

Before the crowd which had gathered on the plain of ʿArafa near the Holy City, the Prophet stood on the hill known as the Mount of Mercy (*Jabal ar-Raḥma*), and delivered his 'Farewell Address', in which he gave his last advice to the community of believers. Several times he repeated: 'Have I accomplished the task?* O Lord God, bear witness!' And each time, the crowd responded with an immense clamour of assent.

The last verse of the Qur'an was revealed on that day:

> *This day have I made perfect for you your religion, and have completed My favour towards you, and am satisfied with Islam for you as your religion.* (v:3)

The Prophet remained in Mecca for only a few days, after which he departed again for Medina. He was now sixty-three, and his health was failing. Sensing that his death was at hand, he gave further words of advice to his Companions, exhorting them especially to practice justice, goodwill and forgiveness. Soon he was unable to lead the congregational prayer, or even to rise to his feet. After several days of suffering, he yielded up his soul. It was the 13th of Rabīʿ, in the Hegira year 11 (8 June 632).

Those who had been close to him were overwhelmed by grief and despair. In the city, the news of the Prophet's death met with consternation; many refused to believe it, or said that Muhammad would soon return and continue to guide his community until the Day of Judgement. At last, Abū Bakr spoke to the crowd which had gathered at the mosque, and declared forcefully that 'Whoever worships Muhammad, let him know that Muhammad has died; but whoever worships God, let him know that God is alive, and does not die.'

* Some writers translate this as: 'Have I delivered the message?'

Then the man who had been the closest friend of the Prophet, and who was to succeed him as the first caliph of Islam, recited the following verse from the Qur'an:

> *Muhammad is but a Messenger; messengers have passed away before him. Shall it be, when he dies, or is slain, that you turn back on your heels? Whoever turns back does God no harm, and God shall reward the thankful.* (III:144)

Having given an overall impression of the public life of Muhammad, a brief glimpse of his private life is doubtless also in order, especially as it has sometimes been the subject, on the part of non-Muslims, of uncomprehending—if not frankly biased—commentaries. To understand his personality one must first appreciate that it was both entirely normal, realising the human condition in its wholeness, and perfectly virtuous. All the sources agree that he was always and unfalteringly truthful, just, good, humble and simple, in addition to exemplifying the qualities of energy and courage which he needed to carry out his mission. While entirely submitted to God, he was in every circumstance master of himself.

While he practiced polygamy, and loved women—as he himself declared—the accusations of sensuality and lust which many Westerners used to direct at him are not credible, and are belied by a number of facts. One must first of all remember that Muhammad was, for more than twenty years, the exemplary husband of a woman fifteen years his senior. He had seven children by her, of whom only one survived him: Fāṭima, who married ʿAlī and became the progenitor of a celebrated line of descendants. After Khadīja's death, he lived for a number of years in complete chastity, and it was only at the age of fifty-three that he began to practice polygamy.

It is unreasonable to pretend, as some Western writers have done, that Muhammad, once installed at Medina, abruptly succumbed to the 'temptations of the flesh'. He had become the head of a community which was constantly growing in influence, and, since he exercised a function which was in a sense that of a patriarch, the majority of the marriages which he entered into were of a political character. These were none the less unions marked by the fullness of his human nature, and he admired feminine beauty. But for him this was an opportunity to give thanks to God, and this, like every aspect of his life, was sacralised by his perfect conformity to the divine order.

Quite apart from the moral dimension of polygamy—a subject to which we shall return in due course—one must see another significance in the Prophet's marriages. As founder of a faith destined to become a great world religion, he was obliged to bequeath examples of conduct which could serve as the basis of the civil legislation of future generations and provide authoritative guidance for all situations. Thus each one of his unions had specific characteristics which, when set with the others, furnished the material for the elaboration of the law which in Islam regulates the relationship between the sexes and lays down norms the stability of which no-one, after fourteen centuries, has been able to challenge. This is one reason why, in accordance with the Revelation, he was able to have nine wives at one time, although in all other cases the Qur'an limits the number to four.

In general one must unhappily concur with an Orientalist like Montgomery Watt when he writes that 'of all the great men of the world, no-one has had as many detractors as Muhammad.' Having engaged in a lengthy study of the life and work of the Prophet, the British Arabist adds that 'it is hard to understand why this has been the case', finding the only plausible explanation in the fact that for centuries Christianity treated Islam as its worst enemy. And although Europeans today look at Islam and its founder in a somewhat more objective light, 'many ancient prejudices still remain.'*

* W.M. Watt, *Muhammad at Medina*. Oxford University Press.

However this may be, 'it is hard', as Professor Seyyed Hossein Nasr puts it, 'for a non-Muslim, particularly if he be the product of a Christian environment, to understand the spiritual significance of the Prophet and his role as prototype of the religious and spiritual life.' This difficulty 'comes from the fact that the spiritual nature of the Prophet is veiled by his human nature, and that his obligations as guide and leader of a human community disguise his specifically spiritual function.'*

On this subject it is also necessary to insist on the fact that Islam does not draw a distinction between 'what is God's' and 'what is Caesar's'. In its perspective, everything belongs to God, and every aspect of human and social life must be sanctified through the legislation and the tradition which proceed directly from the Revelation given to Muhammad, and from his personal example.

Having lived and accomplished his mission by realising perfectly both that which is of this world, and that which relates to the next, the Prophet gave the believers the possibility of fully realising their human condition on earth without for an instant losing their spiritual orientation. In this way he set up the remarkable equilibrium which characterises the man of Islam, and which permits him to taste this earthly life without ever forgetting that we must all return to God and appear before Him. At the same time, he remains the spiritual guide of those people who seach for sanctity, and who discern the most sublime teachings and symbols in everything which he said and did.

With this manifestation, which simultaneously represents primordiality and the totality of the human condition, and which synthesises all the preceding messages from God, the prophetic cycle has been definitively closed. Nothing can be added to this perfect and ultimate Revelation until the Last Judgement.

* Seyyed Hossein Nasr, *Ideals and Realities of Islam*.

SOURCE TEXTS

The prophetic mission

O you who are enveloped in your cloak!
Arise and warn!
Your Lord magnify,
Your raiment purify,
Pollution shun!

Qur'an, LXXIV:1–5

*Yā Sīn.**
By the Wise Qur'an,
Truly you are among those sent,
Along a straight Path.
The revelation of the Mighty, the Merciful,
That you may warn a people whose fathers were not warned,
So they are heedless.

Qur'an, XXXVI, 1–6

*A number of Qur'anic *suras* begin with isolated letters, termed *muqaṭṭaʿāt*, which have been the subject of copious commentaries and conjectures without any really unanimous agreement on their function and significance having been attained. A certain mystery attaches to them, and they are often given an esoteric interpretation. In the two instances cited here, they have given their names to the *sūras* which they inaugurate.

Ṭā Hā.
We have not revealed the Qur'an to you that you might be distressed.
But as a reminder unto him that fears;
A revelation from Him Who created the earth and the high heavens.

Qur'an, XX, 1–4

Thus We send you unto a nation, before whom other nations have passed away, that you may recite to them that which We have inspired in you, as they are disbelievers in the Beneficent. Say: He is my Lord; there is no god save Him. In Him do I put my trust, and unto Him is my recourse.

Qur'an, XIII:30

The first Revelation

The month of Ramaḍān came, and, for the fifth time, Muhammad retreated into solitude on Mount Ḥira. Several weeks passed without incident; and then, on the night before the twenty-seventh day of the month, he received a strange vision: a being of light appeared and spoke to him. As he himself later described it: 'He told me that he was the Angel Gabriel, whom God had sent to inform me that He had chosen me to be His messenger. The angel taught me to perform my ablutions, and when I returned, pure of body, he ordered me to "Read!" "I know not how to read!" I said. He took me into his arms, and held me very tightly, and then, when he released me, ordered me again to read. "But I know not how to read!" I told him. He seized me again, even more severely, and told me to read, and again I told him that I did not know how.

He then took me into his arms for the third time, and crushed me even more violently, and then, releasing me, said:

> *Read! In the name of your Lord Who created,*
> *Created man from a clot of blood.*
> *Read! For your Lord is the Most Generous,*
> *Who has taught through the pen;*
> *Taught man that which he did not know.*

And then the angel departed.

Muhammad Hamidullah, *Le Prophète de l'Islam*

The Imitation of the Prophet

Imitation of the Prophet implies, first, strength as regards oneself, next, generosity as regards others and, thirdly, serenity in God and through God. It could also be said: serenity through piety, in the most profound sense of that term.

Such imitation moreover implies: first, sobriety in relation to the world; secondly, nobility within ourselves in our being; thirdly, truthfulness through God and in Him.

Frithjof Schuon, *Understanding Islam*

The *Miʿrāj*, or 'Night Journey'

The account of the *Miʿrāj* is reported, according to the words of the Prophet himself, by forty-five of his Companions. Confining ourselves to the compilations of Bukhari and Muslim, we learn that the Prophet was at home one night—or, according to another version, in the courtyard of the Kaʿba—when Gabriel came to him to open his chest and wash his heart with water. Then he took him up through the heavens on a celestial mount (*Burāq*, etymologically derived from the same root as *barq*, or lightning). In each of the seven heavens, he presented him to one of the great prophets: Adam, Noah, Moses, Jesus, Abraham, etc. The two then ascended to a point where they could hear the sound of the divine Pen writing the divine decisions and destiny. Gabriel led him on to a certain celestial place, where he indicated the way onwards, not himself possessing the right to go further. Muhammad continued his celestial voyage, and was honoured with the divine audience: God exchanged salutations with him and made him a gift of the daily prayers: the technique of contact. The Prophet passed by the Tree of the Boundary (*Sidrat al-Muntahā*), Paradise and its joys, and Hell and its miseries. On the return journey he paused at Jerusalem, where he was welcomed by all the ancient prophets, and led them in a service of prayer. Then he returned home to Mecca.

Muhammad Hamidullah, *Le Prophète de L'Islam*

4

A miracle and its progressions in history

UNLIKE Christianity, Islam, religion of clarity and certitude, has never attached any essential importance to miracles. Tradition does tell us that Muhammad worked many miracles, but it is not compulsory to set one's faith in them in order to believe that he was truly the Messenger of God invested with the ultimate prophetic mission.

The central miracle of Islam was, and remains, the Qur'anic revelation. To this day no-one has put forward a defensible explanation of how an unlettered caravan merchant of the early seventh century might have been able, by his own devices, to produce a text of such inimitable beauty, of such capacity to stir emotion, and which contained knowledge and wisdom which stood so far above the ideas current among mankind at that time. The studies carried out in the West which try to determine the 'sources used by Muhammad', or to bring to light the psychological phenomenon which enabled him to draw the inspiration from his 'subconscious', have demonstrated only one thing: the anti-Muslim prejudice of their authors.

Although a divine revelation must necessarily transcend human understanding, the process by which each passage of the Qur'an was transcribed into its final and unassailable form was quite clear. Every time a fragment of the text was revealed by the Archangel, the Prophet called one of his Companions and dictated it to him, indicating the place which it occupied in the ensemble of the

Book. Afterwards he would have re-read to him the verses which had just been given him in order to check them. Every year, during the month of Ramaḍān, he recited, as a kind of revision, all that had been revealed to him thus far. This is why it is still the custom in the lands of Islam to recite the entire Qur'an during the Ramaḍān nights.

In the absence of paper the scribes made use of parchment, pieces of leather, wooden tablets, flat stones, even the shoulderblades of camels. After the Prophet's death, these objects were kept by several of his Companions, and variations began to appear. These were eliminated by the Caliph ʿUthmān before they could become the cause of disputes, and, since that time, the Qur'anic text has remained immutable in the form in which it was revealed, a form which has not been the subject of the least controversy. Even today, Muslims in their thousands are able to recite the Qur'an 'by heart'—an expression which is literally correct, since it is the heart, more than the brain, which is penetrated by the Qur'an, whose Arabic original cannot be conveyed by any translation.

Another of Islam's miracles consists in its dazzling expansion during the two centuries which followed the Prophet's death. The rapidity of the Arab conquests, their immense extent, and even more particularly the results achieved, stunned the world and baffle historians, who have frequently stressed their 'impenetrable and mysterious' aspect.

History does, of course, offer other examples of sudden and massive conquest, but in general, all the empires created in this way disintegrated almost as fast as they were born, and scarcely even outlived their founder. Only the empire of Islam stood the test of centuries: the great majority of the lands conquered during the first phases of the expansion remain within its pale today, with regions such as Spain and Sicily, reconquered by Christianity during the Middle Ages, representing no more than marginal exceptions. All of these Muslim territories were of course the scene of many political vicissitudes, but the essential remained. Islam, whose empire was founded far more on the attachment of hearts than on material force, had become rooted deeply and definitively.

Faced with these prodigious military triumphs, which in one century allowed the Muslims to extend their sway over an area extending from China to central France, Christians have often reproached Islam for being a 'religion of the sword,' and of making *jihād*, mistranslated as 'holy war', into an enterprise of conquest and forced conversion. To this, one should first respond that every religion possesses a certain martial quality which appears more or less fully according to historical circumstances, and most especially when the community of believers is under threat. A religion called upon by Providence to be a way to truth and salvation for whole nations cannot fail to make enemies against whom it must fight to maintain itself. Even Buddhist states have had their armies and their wars, while Christianity, whose destiny it was to be the religion of a whole civilisation and of great empires, never hesitated to take up arms against those who stood in its way.

Following the example of the Prophet, who had required Muslim combatants to respect defeated and defenceless enemies, the Muslims, when they were obliged to wage war, attempted to keep it as humane as possible. Their restrained and tolerant attitude went a long way towards winning the sympathy of the populations of the lands where their armies campaigned, and in many regions (such as certain Byzantine provinces) they were welcomed as liberators.

It cannot be claimed that Christian combatants generally showed a greater degree of generosity towards their enemies of other religions. A number of historical examples bear witness to the contrary, particularly during the Crusades. Following the capture of Jerusalem by Godfrey of Bouillon in 1099, his men massacred almost the entire Muslim and Jewish population;

whereas in 638, the caliph Umar had occupied the Holy City without shedding a drop of blood. Similarly, when Saladin recaptured it in 1187 he spared the life of every Christian inhabitant.

In all the lands which it has conquered, Islam has always accepted the presence of numerous and important groups professing other religions. By contrast, when, for instance, the Christians reconquered Spain, all Muslims were massacred, forceably converted, or expelled.

But before the commencement of the massive military campaigns which would subject a large part of the known world to the rule of Islam, the Muslim state was shaken by a crisis which threatened its very existence. This was the *Ridda*, or 'apostasy', which impelled a number of Arab tribes to revolt against Medina under the leadership of an impostor. Abū Bakr, the first caliph, gave the task of subduing the rebellion to Khālid ibn al-Walīd, the same man who had so brilliantly led the Meccan cavalry at Uḥud and who, after his conversion to Islam was named the 'Sword of God'. The matter was soon in hand, rendering the Muslim armies fully available for their great offensives to the north.

These campaigns, which changed the face of the earth, still retain a certain bewildering character which defies the analysis of historians. The Muslim warriors were inferior in every way to the empires which they took on: in numbers, armament, strategy and experience. Their sole superiority consisted in their faith and in their conviction that they were serving the plans of God. It is also true that many of their leaders showed themselves to be generals of exceptional skill. But if a miracle be defined as that which defies rational explanation, then the military triumphs of Islam were miraculous.

The first great conquests were the work of Khālid, that 'Sword of God' who, four years after the Prophet's death, achieved a series of dazzling victories which brought the Byzantine domination of Syria and Palestine to an end, and by the same stroke opened the way to Egypt. Damascus surrendered without a fight, and in 638 Jerusalem capitulated to Umar, who had just succeeded Abū Bakr. When the Caliph arrived it was in the company of a single servant from whom he could hardly be distinguished, and, once he had entered the city, he set an example by respecting the places and sanctuaries of Christian worship.

A little later, another great Muslim general, ʿAmr ibn al-ʿĀṣ, took 4,000 men into Egypt, the population of which was weary of the Byzantine regime. In 642 Alexandria surrendered. In this regard, it should be parenthetically remarked that the legend which accuses the Muslim conquerors of incinerating the famous library is devoid of any truth: it had been dispersed centuries before the Arabs arrived.

Meanwhile, the progress of Islam towards the East was even more impressive. Khālid had already, in 633, occupied an important segment of the territories held by the Sassanid empire in Mesopotamia. The Persian monarch reacted by massing a great army reinforced with elephants. At Qādisiyya, the Muslim general Saʿd ibn Abī Waqqāṣ, after a bitter three-day battle, routed the Persians and penetrated the heart of the Iranian plateau. The Persians assembled a new army, but this was to be their last stand, and they were crushed by al-Nuʿmān at Nihāvend. Qādisiyya, in 637, had assured the Islamic domination of Iraq; Nihāvend in 642 extended it over Persia. In 643, Muslim cavalry stood at the gates of India. Eleven years had passed since the death of the Prophet.

This initial phase of conquest represents Islam's most glorious age, the time of its seamless unity and its full application in the lives of the faithful. It created the *Dār al-Islām* which all later generations of Muslims were to look back upon with nostalgia. Two caliphs, Abū Bakr and ʿUmar, had succeeded to the leadership of the Muslim state. With the third, ʿUthmān (appointed in 644), certain dissensions began to appear, and a number of old Companions, driven by political motives, set themselves in opposition to the Caliph, and in 656 assassinated him.

The tension was further heightened following the designation of ᶜAlī as fourth successor to the Prophet. Under his caliphate a faction withdrew from the majority community: these were the dissidents known as the Khawārij (the 'seceders'), the descendants of whom, relatively few in number, still form a sectarian group in some Muslim countries.

Nevertheless the first four caliphs are generally regarded by Sunnī tradition and piety as 'the rightly-guided' (*rāshidūn*) rulers; and as men endowed with the most incomparable virtue. Countless Muslims have since then borne their names and been inspired by their example. After they were gone, Islam did continue to progress, often in a spectacular fashion, but it had lost its initial unity and coherence.

The conflict which irrupted between ᶜAlī and Muᶜāwiya, the governor of Syria, lies at the root of the great division of Islam into Sunnism and Shīᶜism, a division which still exists today. The Shīᶜa designated themselves as the *shīᶜat ᶜAlī*, the 'faction of ᶜAlī'. The main distinction which separates them concerns the method of succession and the role of the Caliphs. The Shīᶜa believe that these latter must always be descendants of the Prophet and his cousin ᶜAlī, and they attribute to him the mystical function of *imām*, or infallible guide who knows the 'hidden meaning' of the Revelation. Apart from this, however, only minimal differences stand between the two groups, concerning questions of faith, doctrine and religious practice.

The death of ᶜAlī, who was assassinated by a member of the Khawārij, and the accession to the caliphate of Muᶜāwiya, founder of the Umayyad dynasty, did not terminate a conflict which by now had taken on the aspect of a true civil war. Sunni supremacy was reinforced following the battle of Karbalā' in Iraq (680), won by the second Umayyad caliph Yazīd, during which Ḥusayn, the son of ᶜAlī, lost his life in a tragic event which Shīᶜī tradition nurses as a poignant memory.

Remarkably enough, these internal conflicts hardly impinged

on the morale of the Islamic armies which were continuing their conquests in almost every direction at once. From Damascus, where they had established their capital, the Umayyad caliphs found themselves governing an empire in perpetual expansion.

At the outset of the eighth century, the Muslim state took possession of a section of Central Asia, including Khwārazm, Transoxiana and Afghanistan, and reached the borders of China. To the south, it had begun to establish itself on the Indus plain, where a particularly brilliant destiny awaited it.

Similarly impressive was Islam's drive towards the West. Since 643, ʿAmr, conqueror of Egypt, had occupied part of Cyrenaica, and four years later a Muslim army crossed Tripolitania and penetrated Tunis and the old Roman province of 'Africa', which the Arabs thenceforward knew as 'Ifrīqīya'. The country was permanently annexed to the Muslim domain by a nephew of ʿAmr, ʿUqba ibn Nāfiʿ, one of the most outstanding figures of global military history.

Having founded Qayrawān, soon to become one of the foremost centres of Muslim culture in the Maghreb, ʿUqba marched rapidly towards the West and, passing through the interior of Algeria, crossed the Rīf mountains and gained Tangier. From there he headed towards the ancient Roman city of Volubilis, near Meknes, and, continuing to the south, reached the Atlantic at a place not far from Agadir. Tradition tells us that he rode his horse into the waves, and cried: 'I call you to witness, O God, that if there were a way, I would go still further!' He then retraced his steps towards the East.

Obviously, ʿUqba's march was not a conquest which could permit the occupation of the lands which he traversed and in which he had won his victories. But it did allow the Muslims to establish numerous ties with the people of North Africa, where ever since the first contact a certain number of conversions to Islam had taken place. New expeditions, however, were required if North Africa were to be absorbed definitively. This was the work of al-Ḥasan ibn Nuᶜmān, who conquered both Carthage and the famous Kāhina, the priestess who had rallied forces to oppose the Arab occupation in the Aurés mountains. The task was continued by Mūsā ibn Nuṣayr, also one of history's most outstanding generals.

Mūsā had already accomplished a major task of pacification in North Africa when destiny made him into the conqueror of Spain. It is important to note that this conquest, which brought about an Islamic presence on Iberian soil which was to endure for almost eight centuries, was to a great extent the work of recently converted Berbers, led by Ṭāriq ibn Ziyād, the first Muslim leader to cross the straits which ever since have borne his name: the word Gibraltar is derived from Jabal Ṭāriq, the 'Mountain of Ṭāriq.'

During this period, Spain was ruled by a Visigothic king, Roderic, whose power was, however, widely challenged, and who had earned the enmity of a certain Count Julian, a senior figure in the Visigothic regime. Julian persuaded the Muslims to help him depose the king, promising them that they would be welcomed by the populace, and this proved generally the case in most of the regions which they crossed in their drive to the Pyrenees.

Ṭāriq had already, in 710, carried out a raid on the northern shores of the straits, but the first true assault launched by Islam on European territory took place the following year. Near Cadiz, 7,000 Muslims routed almost 25,000 of Roderic's warriors. The Visigothic kingdom put up almost no further resistance, and collapsed. Two years later, all Spain, apart from a strip of territory to the north-west of the peninsula, was conquered. Mūsā, who had joined the campaign in 712, completed the work of his lieutenant by taking possession, in the name of the caliph in Damascus, of the new territory, which, under the name *al-Andalus*, soon developed into one of the most brilliant centres of Arabo-Islamic civilisation.

Following hard on the heels of this spectacular success, the

Muslims continued their thrust and entered France. In 714 their vanguard made a sortie across the Pyrenees, and moved forward to positions outside Avignon and Lyons. The people whom Europe called the 'Saracens' firmly installed themselves at Narbonne, and secured a number of towns in Aquitaine and Provence. Yet at such vast distances from their bases, and given the means available at that time, their thrusts lost something of their initial vigour. In 732 the famous battle of Poitiers took place, from which Charles Martel emerged victorious, thus signalling the end of the Muslim advance in the West.

This famous event was certainly of immense importance, on the symbolic as much as on the military level. But it would be wrong to think that it provoked a rapid reponse which drove all the Arab-Muslim forces from Gaulish soil. For more than two centuries the Saracens retained a presence in some towns of the Midi and the Rhône basin. It was only toward the end of the tenth century that their last stongholds, in the Valais and at La Garde-Freinet on the Provençal coast, were overrun.

Historians and philosophers, both Christian and Muslim, have speculated widely about the events surrounding the Battle of Poitiers and the end of the age of Islamic military expansion. It is undeniable that Christianity came close to total submersion. All the evidence, however, suggests that it was not God's plan that the great Muslim dream of the unification of humanity into one single community of believers should be realised. But until 732 all such hopes appeared to be well-founded, and the warriors of Islam had reason to believe that the dominion of this world, as well as the promise of the next, was guaranteed them. By the time they were forced to switch from an offensive to a more defensive stance the Muslims had become masters of a vast realm whose conquest had been a feat without parallel in history, an event which still retains many facets which defy human reason and allow us justly to speak of it as a prodigy.

Expansion was followed by consolidation. Islam made further

conquests, but often (as in Sicily) these were ephemeral; while at other times gains were no more than a compensation for losses elsewhere. In this way, when the Muslims, at the close of the fifteenth century, were decisively expelled from Spain, they had taken possession of Asia Minor and were penetrating the Balkans, this time with Turkish, not Arab warriors.

Military success may now have been slow in coming, but important progress was made in other directions. The 'kingdom' of Islam, the religion of equilibrium, is a kingdom of this world just as it is of the next; but when conditions in the former fail to favour its operation on a temporal level this does not necessarily obstruct its forward march, since its principal domain is that of the human soul.

Thus Islam penetrated in a entirely peaceful way into numerous Asian countries such as Indonesia (which is now the world's most populous Muslim nation). The huge masses of humanity won for Islam in the Indo-Pakistan subcontinent entered the faith more through spontaneous conversions than as the result of military action. In Africa, the progress of Islam which continues year after year can only be attributed to its radiance and its power to attract.

Equally, it must be recognised that the Islam practised by the majority of believers has been relatively little affected by the events which have marked and often convulsed the political life of the Muslim world throughout its history. It is in this connection that we should now retrace our steps, and recall briefly the evolution of the institution that was the Caliphate.

After making Damascus its seat in 661, the Umayyad caliphate experienced an age of great splendour, not simply in the form of its political success and military triumphs, but also thanks to a sudden and remarkable florescence of civilisation and the arts. This dynasty, a product of the Meccan aristocracy, was none the less faced with an opposition which benefited from the growing pressure of the masses of new converts, who reproached the caliphs for pursuing policies which were too Arab and not sufficiently Muslim. An uprising broke out in the name of the principle that all believers were brothers irrespective of their origins, and this, in 750, swept into power al-Saffāḥ, a descendant of the Prophet's uncle al-ᶜAbbās. The family of the deposed caliph was slaughtered, although one survivor, ᶜAbd ar-Raḥmān, fled westwards and founded the Umayyad caliphate of Cordova. The first Abbasid installed himself at Baghdad, where his dynasty, which lasted for more than five centuries, soon lent an even more lively brilliance to the empire and civilisation of Islam. It is interesting to note that the rival caliphate at Cordova experienced an equally spectacular development in all fields of art and knowledge, compared to which Christian Europe appeared singularly crude and backward.

Among the various factors which led to the enfeebling and then the decadence of this great civilisation, invasions from outside were undoubtedly the most decisive. Muslim Spain was under constant pressure from armies sent by the major kingdoms of Europe which, at the end of the fifteenth century, finally consummated the *Reconquista*. The Crusades, although they ended in defeat for Christianity, also made a significant contribution to the decline of Islam. But it was the Mongol invasion which dealt the most fatal blow.

At the beginning of the thirteenth century the Mongol horsemen of Genghis Khan invaded and laid waste to the most prosperous Asian regions of the Islamic world: Bactria, Khwārazm, Afghanistan, Persia. His successors continued the work of destruction; in 1258, Hülagü entered and sacked Baghdad, where he murdered the Abbasid caliph and his family. Less than two years later it was Syria's turn to endure the catastrophe. Finally, having reached Palestine, the Mongol horde was defeated by the sultan of Egypt, who was himself of Turkish stock.

In a way the conquerers were themselves conquered, as the Mongols gradually adopted Islam, which, at the beginning of the fourteenth century, became the official religion of their state.

When the Turk, Timur Leng (Tamberlaine), who regarded himself as the heir and successor of Genghis Khan, left on his campaigns, he claimed to be fighting for Sunni orthodoxy. This did not prevent him, however, from perpetrating the most horrific massacres and devastation in the lands which he overran, not sparing in any way the populations which professed the same faith. His passage through Aleppo and Damascus (1400–1401) left terrible memories.

At the dawn of the modern period, four states formed important empires in the lands of Islam and remained powerful enough to hold their own against a Europe which by now was in full expansion.

Firstly there were the Ottoman Turks, who had occupied Constantinople (Istanbul) in 1453, transforming it into their capital, and whose monarch had assumed the title of Caliph. They extended their authority over the whole Near and Middle East, including most of the Arabian peninsula and the Holy Cities of Arabia, together with the Arab countries of the Mediterranean littoral (with the exception of Morocco). The Ottoman Empire also annexed vast areas populated by Christians, particularly in the Balkans, but, sliding into a condition of senile decadence, was unable to withstand the shock of the First World War, in which it took the side of Germany, and which ended with its dismemberment.

On the Eastern flank of the Turks, the Shīʿite dynasty of the Safavids had constituted, since the beginning of the sixteenth century, a powerful state whose influence beyond its frontiers, particularly in the area of literature and the arts, was at times very considerable. It was the founder of the Safavid dynasty, Shāh Ismāʿīl, who made Persia into the principal citadel of Shīʿism in the Muslim world, a status which it has retained to the present day.

Further to the east, a great conqueror by the name of Babur, a descendant of Timur Leng by his father and of Genghis Khan by his mother, became the first in the illustrious line of Moghul emperors, extending his power over Afghanistan and Northern India. The Indo-Muslim empire which he thus founded knew a splendour which dazzled the European travellers who saw it, and survived, at least on paper, until the proclamation of the British Indian Empire in the middle of the last century.

Finally, at the extreme west of the Muslim world (*al-Maghrib al-Aqṣā*), Europe had an important neighbour in the reasonably powerful state of Morocco. During the seventeenth century, power came into the hands of the Sherifian dynasty of the Alawites, which has remained in place until the present. Particularly brilliant was the reign of Mawlay Ismāʿīl (1672–1727), who expelled the Europeans from all the Moroccan lands which they had occupied (with the exception of Ceuta), and bequeathed to us some of the finest monuments of North African art.

It is routine among historians and orientalists to assert that since the end of the Middle Ages, Islam dwelt in a state of lethargy from which it awoke only on the advent of the modern period following contact with the West. This opinion is justified, at least in part, if we consider the political and military decline of most Muslim states, together with the overall degeneration of intellectual, scientific and artistic activity, but it is hard to reconcile with the evidence which shows that the faith of the Prophet has continued, ever since the beginning of modern times, to progress and win the loyalty of sizeable sections of humanity, in Asia, and—most substantially—in Africa.

The facts show clearly that these conversions to Islam were not commonly the result of force, but were more the consequence of a magnetic power radiating from the Muslim community itself and from some of its representatives. Many religious brotherhoods, animated by shaykhs who were regarded as saints, exercised a luminous attraction for many souls engaged in the quest for new certainties.

In this respect it is fascinating to note the following contrast. In the vast area of the Balkans which they had appended to their empire, the Ottomans usually respected the Qur'anic injunction which states that *there shall be no compulsion in religion* (II:256), so that conversions remained, on the whole, very few on the ground. By contrast, in a country such as Indonesia, where the presence of Islam never took on a military aspect but was imported peacefully by merchants from India and southern Arabia, progress was swift, with the result that Indonesia is today the world's largest Muslim country.

Spreading through all the Malay peoples, by the end of the fourteenth century Islam had reached the Philippines, where it made the most progress in the southern islands. When the Spaniards arrived in the sixteenth century they were forced to fight against Muslims as they had done in their own country and in North Africa. The colonialist expeditions and conquests made in the Orient and Africa by the European powers during this period had as one of their imperial purposes the weakening of Islam, the influence of which they vigorously strove to counteract.

None the less, even during the great periods of their colonial expansion, Westerners were never able to thwart seriously what they termed Muslim 'infiltration' into new geographic areas. Islam, which had gained a certain influence in China at the beginning of modern times, now acquired footholds in Burma and Indochina. It penetrated—again peacefully—into Sri Lanka, where its followers today form an important and active minority.

Although the situation in Asia seems to have been roughly stable for the last century, this has not been so in Africa, where Islam has been able to achieve spectacular progress and, over vast areas stretching more and more towards the south, has thwarted the efforts of the Christian missions, despite the incomparably greater material resources at their disposal. It is not possible even to guess at any statistics for a phenomenon of this kind, but the Muslim advance is sufficiently well attested to by Christian sources for its general character and volume to be well established as fact.

It should finally be pointed out that Islam is not entirely absent even from the Americas. The most compact group lives in Surinam (the former Dutch Guiana), where a quarter of the population of some 340,000 consists of Muslims of Indonesian, Indian or African origin. A relatively important number of Syrian and Lebanese Muslims live in Brazil and Argentina, while in the United States a conversion movement has appeared among the black population (the 'Black Muslims', and a range of other groups).

There is a further event of importance in Islamic history which remains to be discussed.

As we have said, the Ottoman sultan bore the title of Caliph. After the defeat of 1918 and the revolution which it unleashed, the Turkish National Assembly abolished first the monarchy, and then the institution of the Caliphate (1924). The event provoked reverberations and protest movements, particularly in India, where the Muslims held Europe responsible for the destruction of this traditional Islamic institution. The attempt made a little later by the Sherif Hussein of the Hijaz to claim the title miscarried, and has never been repeated.

Thus ended the long line of caliphs, who had succeeded one another since the earliest days of Islam. Many Muslims still lament their passing, and, even if on the strictly religious level the disappearance of the caliphal function has not generated any of the serious consequences which might have been expected, there are some people who have not entirely given up the idea of a restoration.

Although this institution had become devoid of real substance, its end in a way marked the consummation of the political abasement of an Islam which, since the nineteenth century, had in many regions submitted to the colonial dominion of European powers of Christian origin. In fact the aggression of which the

Muslim peoples were the victims had nothing in common with the spirit of the Crusades—for its motive power issued exclusively from the materialist preoccupations of modern secular civilisation. It was this, however, which made it especially pernicious, since it did not confine itself to frontal, direct attacks, as the Crusaders and Mongols had done, but instead injected the insidious poison of 'progressist' ideas which, in spite of certain appearances, were fundamentally opposed to Islam as a doctrine of truth and a path to salvation. Put differently, whereas during the Middle Ages the enemies of Islam slew the flesh by committing physical massacres, in the modern age they did violence to souls.

The above remarks may help us to understand why modern movements of 'Islamic rebirth' tend to be somewhat ambiguous and equivocal. Happily dubbing themselves the vanguard of a *nahḍa*, an 'awakening', or 'renewal', they lay claim to the glorious past of an Islam whose brilliance they long to restore, and yet at the same time have a tendency to believe that the modern ideology of 'progress', which developed far outside the Islamic context, might favour their ambitions; so much so that at times they go to the extent of subjecting their thinking entirely to the historico-social conceptions of the post-Christian West.

Certainly, the end of the colonial empires and protectorates, a just conclusion to long and painful struggles for freedom, brought elation to all Muslim hearts, although the 'mutations' which accompanied or followed it often did no more than to accentuate the ideological supremacy of the West, the physical and political domination of which had so rightly been rejected. Liberation is still far from being achieved, and, in the continent of Asia, vast areas with an ancient Islamic culture remained until very recently in subjection to a colonial system which was only now been cast aside.

It is hard to estimate the Muslim population of the former Soviet Union. In any case, the figure of 30 million which is most usually given represents a minimum, and it is more than likely that the real number is now substantially higher. One can, however, ask whether, rather than being Muslims in the full sense of the term, it might not be more accurate to speak of many of them as 'people of Muslim ancestry', who to a greater or lesser extent were forced to abandon all the practices of their religion. The Soviet regime never faltered in its direct and violent persecution of Islam, despite the tolerance which religion theoretically enjoyed from the state. None the less, the unremitting fury of the official propaganda which was until very recently hurled against Islam seems itself to bear witness to its continuing vitality. Meanwhile the worldwide Muslim community cares but little for these 'fraternal' peoples of Central Asia, who are certainly as deserving of their sympathy and solidarity as anyone else.

By contrast, the Palestinian problem continues to hold Muslim attention, and it is true that there is no shortage of reasons for this. The Zionist movement has in practice always been more or less anti-Muslim, and the state which it created is not merely a source of propaganda and policies hostile to Islam, but, thanks to its potent war machine built up by American industry, also represents a direct threat to the countries and peoples who form the heart of Islam, and even to their holy places.

In his *Annuaire du monde musulman*, published in 1954, Louis Massignon put the total population of the world community of Islam at 365 million. Writing more than a quarter of a century later, the celebrated Orientalist Louis Gardet (in his work *L'Islam, hier—demain*, published in collaboration with Mohammed Arkoun), raised this figure to 800 million. Has the number of Muslims in the world really doubled in such a short space of time? It is not easy to credit this; one is more inclined to think that Massignon's figure was an underestimate. None the less, a fair number of Muslims now regard even the figure of 800 million as being too low. The Muslim World League, the headquarters of which is at Mecca, calculates that a more just figure would be around one billion.

However this may be, such arithmetic is less than important, since Islam and the outlook which it engenders always lay emphasis on the qualitative aspect of things, in contrast to modern civilisation, one of the chief characteristics of which is to be quantitative and to be satisfied with statistics. What must be recalled above all else is that this religion, which has proceeded from the final revelation of the cosmic cycle, is experiencing in our time an expansion corresponding to its providential vocation. In this dark age it yields the last rays of declining day, as an expression of the *raḥma*, the divine mercy, which shall remain accessible to men until the very end.

In any case, if Islam today appears to be progressing with regard to the number of its adherents, it remains irreconcilably in opposition to 'this world'. Probably it even represents the most significant force of resistance to the subversive trends of modern secular civilisation.

In this regard, Muslims must none the less harbour no illusions about the influence which they may wield over the course of events, since the Prophet once said in a *ḥadīth*: 'At the end, Islam shall be much enfeebled in the earth.' 'Shall the Muslims be few in number at that time?' he was asked, and he replied: 'No, they shall be numerous indeed, but they shall be powerless in the face of their enemies.'

According to another *ḥadīth*, Islam, at the end, will be 'a stranger in the world', as it was at its beginning. But, as the Prophet added, happy shall be those strangers who seek to remedy the misdeeds of men.

SOURCE TEXTS

Fight!

Fight against those who have been given the Book and who believe not in God or the Last Day, and forbid not that which God has forbidden by His messenger, and follow not the religion of Truth, until they pay the tribute readily, being brought low. Qur'an, IX:29

O you who believe! When in battle you meet those who disbelieve, do not turn your backs to them. Whoever on that day turns his back to them, unless manoeuvering for the fight or attempting to join a company, has incurred the wrath of God, and his dwelling-place shall be Gehenna, an evil journey's end. Qur'an, VIII:15–6

Do not say of those who were killed in the way of God that they are dead. Rather they are alive, but you perceive it not. Qur'an, II:154

Appeal to the People of the Book (Jews, Christians, Sabeans)

Say: O people of the Book! Come to an agreement between us and you: that we shall worship none save God, and ascribe no partners unto Him, and that none of us shall take others for lords beside God. And if they turn away, then say: bear witness that we are Muslims. Qur'an, III:64

Do not dispute with the people of the Book, unless it be in a way that is better, save with such of them as do wrong; and say: We believe in that which has been revealed unto us, and revealed unto you; our God and your God is One, and unto Him we surrender.

Qur'an, XXIX:46

Among the people of the Book there are some who believe in God and that which is revealed unto you and that which was revealed unto them, humbling themselves before God. They do not sell the revelations of God for a trifling gain. Their reward is with their Lord, and God is swift to take account.

Qur'an, III:199

The best community

You are the best community to have been raised up for mankind. You enjoin what is right, and forbid what is wrong, and you believe in God. If the people of the Book had believed it would have been better for them. Some of them are believers, but most of them are corrupt.

Qur'an, III:110

The Qur'an: a fact humanly inexplicable

Since I had now seen the wide gap separating the reality of Islam from the image we have of it in the West, I experienced a great need to learn Arabic (which I did not speak) to be sufficiently well-equipped to progress in the study of such a misunderstood religion. My first goal was to read the Qur'an, and to make a sentence by sentence analysis of it with the help of various commentaries essential to a critical study. My approach was to pay special attention to the description of numerous natural phenomena given in the Qur'an; the highly accurate nature of certain details referring to them in the Book, which was only apparent in the original, struck me by the fact that they were in keeping with present-day ideas, although a man living at the time of Muhammad could not have suspected this at all. I subsequently read several works written by Muslim authors on the scientific aspects of the Qur'anic text; they were extremely helpful in my appreciation of it, but I have not so far discovered a general study of this subject made in the West.

What initially strikes the reader confronted for the first time with a text of this kind is the sheer abundance of subjects discussed: the Creation, astronomy, the explanation of certain matters concerning the earth, and the animal and vegetable kingdoms, human reproduction. Whereas monumental errors are to be found in the Bible, I could not find a single error in the Qur'an. I had to stop and ask myself: If a man was the author of the Qur'an, how could he have written facts in the seventh century AD that today are shown to be in keeping with modern scientific knowledge? There was absolutely no doubt about it: the text of the Qur'an we have today is most definitely a text of that period, if I may be allowed to put it in these terms . . .. What human explanation can there be to this observation? In my opinion there is no explanation; there is no special reason why an inhabitant of the Arabian Peninsula should, at a time when King Dagobert was reigning in France (629–39 AD), have had scientific knowledge on certain subjects that was ten centuries ahead of our own.

Maurice Bucaille, *The Bible, the Quran and Science*

No-one was converted by the sword

The concept of the dissemination of Islam by the sword must really be abandoned (that is, for the earliest era of the Arab diaspora), since a critical study of sources has shown that the victorious Arabs never presented the people they had conquered with the choice between death and the acceptance of their faith. When the Muslims had dealings with the 'people of the Book' (Christians and Jews) they did not offer them this choice, but simply made them subject peoples and exacted tribute money from them, following the instructions of the Revelation. In the practice of war, the Zoroastrians of Persia, and later the Indian Brahmans and Buddhists of the Punjab—among whom the Arabs appeared victorious—were soon assimilated into the category of the Jews and Christians of Syria, Palestine, Egypt and Africa. The alternative between Islam and death was only given to pagan idolators, with whom the Arabs had dealings very rarely in that early period of their activities outside Arabia. Thus, the straight indoctrination of their defeated enemies never seems to have been the major concern of the Arab conquerors.

Francesco Gabrieli, *Muhammad and the Arab Conquests*

Respect for conquered peoples

The conduct of the caliph Umar at Jerusalem shows us the mildness with which the Arab conquerors treated the vanquished, and contrasts vividly with the actions of the Crusaders in the same city several centuries later. Umar wanted to enter the Holy City with only a small number of his companions. He asked the Patriarch Sophronius to accompany him on the visit which he wished to make to the sites consecrated by religious tradition, and then declared to the inhabitants that they were safe, that their property and churches would be respected, and that the Muslims would not make their prayers in Christian churches.

Amr's conduct in Egypt was no less benign. To its inhabitants he offered complete religious freedom, impartial justice for all, the inviolability of property, and the replacement of the arbitrary and excessive taxes of the Greek emperors by an annual tribute fixed at 15 dirhams per capita. The inhabitants of the provinces showed themselves so satisfied with these offers that they lost no time in agreeing to the treaty, and paid the tribute in advance. So religiously did the Arabs respect the conventions which were accepted, so agreeable did they make themselves to the populations which earlier had been subjected to the vexations of the Christian agents of the emperor at Constantinople, that all Egypt adopted their religion and their language with enthusiasm. This, it must be reiterated, was a result which could not have been achieved through force. Not one of the peoples who had ruled Egypt before the Arabs had accomplished this.

Gustave Le Bon, *La Civilisation des Arabes*

5

What one must believe and do to be a Muslim

UNITY, the primary concept of Islam, implies totality. The religion which drives man to unity necessarily includes everything which makes up his life. Islam would contradict itself were it to leave anything out of its orbit.

Islam thus governs all of human existence, as much on the individual as on the collective level. In all the rules which it comprises, all the rites which it prescribes, the whole style which it impresses on the forms and activities of life, there remains present in one way or another, and to varying degrees, the fundamental intention: to gather multiplicity into unity, or—what amounts to the same thing—the periphery into the centre.

Here again, Islam is the precise antithesis of the quantitative modern culture which, oriented towards fragmentation and the marginal, is an alienation and a denial of unity, which it manifests primarily in the caricature which is uniformity. Everything in the modern world is characterised by the spirit of division (*diabolos*, the Greek etymological origin of the word 'Devil', which Arabic made into *Iblīs*, meaning, literally, 'the disuniter'); even the atom, thus named by the ancients to signify 'that which is indivisible', has been smashed and split, with the traumatic consequences with which we are all so familiar. Man, in this 'age of conflicts', who is ever more incapable of living in harmony with his fellow men, is also ever more frequently divided against himself, and is unable to find any inner peace in this world, in which everything leads to the external, where nothing gathers, but all disperses.

The practice of Islam provides solid and effective means of resisting this movement of disintegration which leads both man and society to ruination. Its traditional rules and usages all comprise, in one way or another, a reference back to unity. They also make the Muslim life a constantly renewed recollection of the One, something to which life in the modern secularised world is systematically oblivious, being dissipated in multiplicity in a way which is at once organised and chaotic.

Muslim worship rests upon five main duties, termed the 'pillars' (*arkān*) of Islam: the confession of faith (*shahāda*), the ritual prayer (*ṣalāt*), the Ramadan fast (*ṣawm*), the statutory alms (*zakāt*), and the pilgrimage (*ḥajj*).

The confession of faith occupies a central position in relation to the other four canonical duties, which are, in a sense, merely its effects or applications in the life of the believers and the community. It comprises a witnessing, or attestation, that 'there is no divinity save God, and that Muhammad is the Messenger of God' (*lā ilāha illa'Llāh, Muḥammadun rasūlu'Llāh*). The act of uttering this formula determines definitively and irrevocably the condition of being Muslim, and of belonging to the *Umma*.

In the practice of Islam, the *shahāda* does not take the form of a definite rite, but instead punctuates the whole of Muslim life as a constant reminder of the unity and omnipotence of God. It is repeated in the ear of newborn infants, and a man on his deathbed must make himself say it for as long as he can, while those who are present repeat it to him until his last breath. It is proclaimed by the muezzins who, five times each day, summon the faithful to prayer. It is also recited frequently while performing other rites, and it is not unusual for particularly fervent or mystical Muslims to repeat it ceaselessly in their minds, never losing for a moment the state of recollection (*dhikr*) of the sole Reality.

The condition of being Muslim requires, apart from the attestation of the *shahāda*, adherence to an array of articles of faith, or 'necessary beliefs', which flow from it more or less directly.

Firstly, the recognition of God's Unity (*tawḥīd*) implies belief in His attributes: Creator, Omnipotent, Omniscient, Absolutely Transcendent, to Whom nothing can be compared or associated, Who possesses all the qualities which symbolically express the names by which He is described in revelation, and which are entirely contained in the first and most essential of them all: *Allāh*.

Next, Islam requires that one believe in the Angels, the revealed Books, and the Prophets who delivered the divine message. These elements of Muslim faith are summarised in a frequently cited verse:

> *The Messenger believes in that which is sent down to him from his Lord, as do the believers. All have faith in God, His Angels, His Books and Messengers. We make no distinction between any of His messengers. They said: 'We hear and obey'.* (11:285)

Among revealed texts, Muslim orthodoxy explicitly recognises the authenticity of the Torah (the Pentateuch), the Psalms and the Gospel, but considers that these Jewish and Christian scriptures have over the years undergone serious deformations which have altered their meaning. It does not exclude the possibility that the books of other religions, such as those of Asia, go back to an ancient divine origin.

As we noted in Chapter 3, Muhammad, 'Seal of the Prophets', brought to a close the long series of Messengers who had come either to proclaim the timeless message of the divine Truth to men, or to remind them of it. It is thus a duty not only to believe in these Prophets, of whom several are mentioned in the Qur'an, but to have faith in *Mūsā* (Moses) and *ᶜĪsā* (Jesus) in particular.

Muslims thus believe in the divine mission of the 'son of Mary', born without human intervention, but reject the idea of the incarnation, considering it a sin of 'association' (*shirk*) to worship him as a divine being or to call him the 'son of God', for he was but a servant and messenger, like the other Prophets. Moreover, Islam does not acknowledge that Jesus was slain by men; instead, only the likeness of his body was crucified. It does teach, however, that he was taken up to Heaven, whence he must return among mankind at the end of time. As for the Virgin Mary (*Maryam*), she is also the object of especial veneration by Muslims, who include her among the Prophets.

To believe in the Day of Judgement and in just retribution for the actions which we have made during our earthly lives is one of the articles of faith on which Islam places the most insistence, as we have already pointed out. According to Muslim eschatology, this ultimate denouement will be preceded by a series of disastrous and terrifying events. God shall then manifest Himself as *King of Judgement-day*, as He is termed in the Opening *Sūra* of the Qur'an, which is recited by the faithful during every one of their daily prayers, and all men shall be resurrected to appear before Him. Ranked behind their Prophet, the Muslims will find him an especially effective intercessor.

The just will go to Paradise, where every joy shall be accorded them for ever, although closeness to God shall be the supreme climax and the most excellent reward which shall surpass any joy which could be imagined. Hell shall be the retribution of the unjust, although according to the most widespread opinion in Muslim theology, all sins shall finally be forgiven, with the exception of the unbelief of those who obstinately refused to recognise the Divine Unity.

To the list of beliefs necessary for one to be Muslim, one must add predestination (*qadar*), which has already been dealt with in Chapter 2 in connection with the idea of liberty. This concerns the alleged 'fatalism' of the faith, which, in reality, is simply equivalent to the fundamental attitude of *islam*: submission to God, Whose will is superior always to that of men. The whole of

Islamic history shows that consciousness of the divine decree which governs all things here on earth does not in any way rule out human effort, and that to accept a destiny willed by Heaven is not the same as passivity.

These, very briefly summed up, are the principal constituent elements of Muslim faith (*īmān*). They are generally accepted, without being the subject of major controversy, by all members of the *Umma*. Only by rejecting them—in practice a very rare occurrence—can one forfeit the state of being Muslim which, in theory, is retained even by those who do not observe the practical obligations of the faith.

Worship, the corollary of the acceptance of belief, finds its principal expression in the ritual prayer (*ṣalāt*), the second 'pillar' of Islam. This is an indispensable and fundamental religious duty which constitutes the only real liturgy of Muslim worship. Its performance imposes a strict and relatively exacting discipline which marks all of life with its sacred rhythm, and, from dawn to night, brings the believer before God and prevents him from being submerged in material and worldly concerns.

The act of worship which is the *ṣalāt*, which some translators render not as 'prayer' but as 'service', must be carried out in a state of ritual purity. To this end, ablutions are prescribed, major or minor (*ghusl* or *wuḍū'*) as the case may be. There are other prescriptions which concern the cleanliness of the worshipper's body and clothes, and also of the place in which he observes his ritual obligation. These requirements are all endowed with symbolic and spiritual meaning; on a more material and practical level they contribute substantially to individual and collective hygiene.

Proclaimed from atop the minarets by the muezzin's cry, all prayers are observed in congregation, although in actual fact large numbers of people attend only the Friday prayer, which—at least for men—is a canonical obligation. Everyone is free to observe the others at home, at work, or anywhere he may happen to be, although it is recommended to perform them in a mosque, which means that in a Muslim society which remains sufficiently traditional, prayer is not only integrated into life, but defines its whole rhythm.

The morning prayer (*ṣubḥ*) is observed at first light, the second (*ẓuhr*) immediately after the sun has passed its meridian, the third (*ᶜaṣr*) in the mid-afternoon, the fourth (*maghrib*) after sunset, and the fifth and last (*ᶜishā'*) at nightfall.

It should be noted that this succession of ritual acts which set man in front of God incorporates a rhythm which is cosmic, not only because it follows the natural movement of the sun, but also because of the acceleration which it entails. The interval between each prayer diminishes as the day advances, the longest period being that between *ṣubḥ* and *ẓuhr*, while the shortest is between *maghrib* and *ᶜishā'*. This same universal acceleration is perceptible in the lives of us all, and the phenomenon which may be termed the 'acceleration of history' is also a clear manifestation of it. It is expressed by the Qur'an itself: the longest chapters come at the opening of the Sacred Book, while at the end we find the shortest, which are also those which, in increasingly breathless cadences, insist on the impermanence of this world and the imminent advent of the Last Hour.

In this way, the Muslim who discharges his ritual obligations not only performs an act of worship which expresses his submission to God, but also brings himself into harmony with the circle of uninterrupted prayer which is centred on the Kaᶜba of Mecca, since somewhere on the globe it is always time to pray, and, in this way, for fourteen centuries, the Muslim masses have not ceased for an instant to entreat the Almighty by reciting the words of the *Fātiḥa*, the first chapter of the Qur'an, which is the principal component of the prayer-rite:

Praise be to God, Lord of the Worlds,
the Compassionate, the Merciful,
King of Judgement-day!

> *You alone do we worship;*
> *to You alone do we turn for help.*
> *Guide us along the straight path,*
> *the path of those whom You have favoured,*
> *not of those against whom there is wrath,*
> *nor of those who go astray.*

The *ṣalāt*, which is not a mere cerebral operation, but engages the whole being of the believer, involves four main positions: standing upright, bowing, prostrating, and sitting on the heels. Each is redolent with symbolic and spiritual messages which have provided the subject matter for countless traditional commentaries. According to one of the most popular, the Islamic prayer synthesises the forms of submission and worship of all created beings: the trees and the mountains stand upright, the stars rise and set, the animals are bowed, and every living thing draws its nourishment from the earth. Through the *ṣalāt*, then, the believer reinstates the central position in creation for which God has destined man. It is only superficial spirits who see in these movements and positions nothing more than a formalism whose meaning eludes them, or a kind of gymnastic exercise which—one is forced to admit—is surely excellent for the health.

The Muslim—man or woman—who for any reason is prevented from observing the prayer at the prescibed time, can simply make it up later. For Islam is designed to adapt to all circumstances, and, in granting it to mankind, God did not wish to impose a burden too heavy, and instead took abundant account of human frailty.

It must be added that Muslim piety knows other forms of prayer over and above the canonical obligation of the *ṣalāt*. It is customary, after finishing the *ṣalāt*, to address oneself to God in individual prayer and supplication (*duʿā'*) in which the believer entreats His support or gives expression to his ardour. There exists also a vast number of formulas, frequently drawn from the

Qur'an, which are repeated with a set of beads; and there are also various litanies of praises and blessings to be invoked upon the Prophet.

Lastly, a characteristic practice of Islam is *dhikr* (literally, 'remembrance', or 'mention'), which consists of the repetition, sometimes rhythmic, of a sacred phrase or, more simply, of the divine Name of God, pronounced at devout gatherings, or, on an individual basis, in all the circumstances of life. There is a sense in which the whole practice of Islam is, in one form or another, *dhikr*: the remembrance of God. There are reasons for believing, too, that this unceasing invocation on the part of the Muslim community provides all humanity with benefits which are incomparably preferable to those of 'progress' or 'development', and which, should it ever be silenced, would in all probability signal the destruction of the world.

The fast (*ṣawm*) of the month of Ramaḍān, the third 'pillar', is a particularly demanding duty which imposes on the members of the community a discipline and self-control which are genuinely difficult, and completely at variance with the self-indulgent orientation of the modern mind. It consists of a total abstention, from before dawn until sunset, from eating, drinking, smoking, using perfumes, and sexual activity.

This abstinence, however, comes to an end as soon as the muezzin announces the *maghrib* prayer from the minaret. The nights of Ramaḍān often turn into parties at which people eat to their hearts content, until the instant comes when it is possible to *'distinguish a white from a black thread at dawn'*.* This, however, hardly lessens the difficulties of the abstention itself, particularly when the days are long and hot, and when the body must be denied all the things to which it is accustomed. In any case, in order to know accurately the rigour of the practice, it is necessary to have experienced it personally. It is hard not to

* This is a Qur'anic expression (11:187). The fast actually begins at the moment when one can discern the line of the eastern horizon.

admire the fact that the Islamic peoples continue so generally to submit to it.

The spiritual—and even material—advantages of the fast are as substantial as its practice is demanding. In particular, it sets up a momentary abolition of man's dependance on his link with the world of matter, and thereby restores his connection with God. By breaking the routine of his daily, terrestrial life, it provides every man with an opportunity to control his instincts. Although it is a duty based on obedience and austerity which brings one closer to God, the Ramaḍān fast is not without a social impact, since it submits both rich and poor to the same privations, with the result that according to traditional custom, Islamic solidarity is especially evident during the sacred month, when it takes the form of special alms and other forms of generosity towards the deprived.

Although as a general rule the practice of the fast is beneficial to the health, there are canonical dispensations which ease matters for those who are sick, pregnant, on a journey, or who are obliged to make an effort connected with the *jihād*. Those who avail themselves of this concession, however, are obliged to make up the days lost by fasting an equivalent number of days later in the year; or, if they cannot, by giving substantial sums in charity, the value of which has been laid down by tradition.

It is also important to realise that in view of the lunar calendar employed in Islam, the month of Ramaḍān moves forward steadily by about ten or twelve days annually in relation to the solar calendar. Thus it moves through all the seasons in every geographic region of the earth, which has the effect of dividing fairly the rigours of the fast between the Muslim populations living north and south of the equator.

Similarly, the theologians and jurists have laid down special arrangements to be observed in the regions near the poles, where, in summer, the short nights can make the fast difficult to sustain. One of the solutions most frequently adopted consists in using the timings effective at the 45th parallel as a basis and applying them to all higher latitudes.

Inevitably, minds interested only in 'productivity' and the quantitative norms of 'development' denounce the practice of fasting as 'anti-economic', being blind to the immense spiritual and qualitative benefits which flow from it. The Soviet authorities in particular always enforced repressive measures against Muslims who persisted in fasting.

In many Islamic countries, however, it can be a punishable offence to eat, drink or smoke in public during the daylight hours when the entire population is abstaining from these things. While there are obviously many people who abide by this discipline without internalising its significance, merely to conform to public custom, there are many others who remain aware that the fast of Ramaḍān constitutes one of the most simple and effective means by which men may escape enslavement to matter and to animality.

The principal sense of of the word *zakāt*, the 'pillar' which is the mandatory alms-tax, is 'purification'. In effect, one does purify oneself by giving away one's possessions (cf. XCII:18), and this too amounts to a sacrifice which annuls the malevolence of the excessively quantitative aspect of man's earthly goods by making them participate in the eminently qualitative sanctity which Islam bestows upon all of life.

In practice, none the less, the *zakāt* is mainly an expression of solidarity: a characteristically Muslim virtue. It must be paid by individual Muslim citizens, and is, in principle, made over to social aid, in distinction to the *jizya*, the poll tax levied from members of the other religious communities, which is paid into the public treasury and is used to cover state expenditure.

In traditional Islamic societies, the institution of *zakāt*, which relies on either governmental or community administration, conforms precisely to the instructions of the Qur'an:

> *The alms are only for the poor and the needy, and those who work to collect them, and those whose hearts are to be reconciled, and to free captives and debtors, and for the cause of God, and for the wayfarer; as a duty imposed by God. Truly, God is the All-Knowing, the All-Wise.* (IX:60)

This text indicates clearly the objectives of the social solidarity associated with the *zakāt*, which gives priority to the most deprived. Even though the revenues of this form of fiscal legislation may also be used for the propagation of Islam, it should be noted that non-Muslims who are in need may at times be included among the beneficiaries of this financial assistance, even though it is paid exclusively by Muslims.

The traditional schools of law have laid down all the details which govern the way in which *zakāt* is to be paid. It is payable on the following categories of wealth: gold and silver, commercial merchandise and profits (at the rate of two and a half percent), and on agricultural produce and livestock (ten percent).

In the majority of Muslim states today, *zakāt* is collected by the taxation departments along with other, purely secular taxes. Inevitably this has caused it to lose some of its charitable and sacred character. But payment of the *zakāt al-fiṭr* at the end of Ramaḍān remains a religious duty which few Muslims fail to observe. Many believers also practice solidarity and charity in numerous other forms of voluntary almsgiving which are more or less fixed by tradition, being inspired by the Qur'anic verse which declares: *If you lend God an excellent loan, He will double it for you, and will grant you His forgiveness* (LXIV:17).

The pilgrimage to Mecca, the fifth 'pillar' of Islam (often it is put in fourth place, before the *zakāt*), means many things. Above all, however, it is a Return to the Centre. For the Kaʿba of Mecca, which Muslims look upon as the centre of the world, is in a way the projection onto this earth of the absolute Centre which is God.

By discharging the duty of making a physical visit to the holy place to which he constantly turns in prayer, the Muslim gives concrete expression to the aspiration which drives him to draw nearer to God. The Kaʿba itself is designated the 'House of God', and yet all are aware that it is empty and contains nothing visible. This should serve as a timely reminder to the pilgrim that what matters is the spiritual return, of which the voyage to Mecca is no more than the symbolic expression; it may, too, explain the fact that the *ḥajj* is not obligatory to the same degree as the other 'pillars', being indispensable only for those Muslims who possess the material means to perform it.

Every believer who reaches Mecca has a sense of a journey achieved from the periphery to the Centre, the locus of Unity. At the same time, however, he affirms the unity of the Islamic universe. This is because the pilgrims, who represent the very greatest diversity of races and peoples, have only one nationality, that of the *umma*, at the moment of their approach to the *ḥaram*, the sanctuary which surrounds the Kaʿba. Everything which had distinguished and divided them is annihilated, since every man is wearing the *iḥrām*, a ritual garment made of two pieces of coarse, white, seamless fabric; while women, their faces uncovered, are also garbed in white.

Everyone repeats the same invocation which the Prophet and his Companions pronounced when they approached the Kaʿba fourteen centuries ago, and which has been repeated by all pilgrims since that time: *Labbayk Allāhumma labbayk* . . . 'Here I am, O Lord, here I am! No partner have you, here I am! Yours is the praise and the grace, yours the kingdom! No partner have You!'

The actual performance of the pilgrimage involves a series of rites which are charged with profound metaphysical and symbolic meaning, and most of which are far older than Islam itself. The first of these is the *ṭawāf*, the seven circuits of the Kaʿba, which mark the arrival at the Centre and constitute the homage which is its due. It is followed by the *saᶜy*, a rapid walk between the two hillocks of Ṣafā and Marwa (today included within the boundaries of the *ḥaram*), and which commemorates the desperate search of Hagar, the wife of Abraham, for water for her son Ishmael, who was in danger of dying of thirst in the desert until he was saved by the miraculous gushing forth of the Zamzam well, which has never since ceased to flow.

It is on the plain of ᶜArafa, however, at the foot of the Mount of Mercy (*Jabal al-Raḥma*), that the culminating rites of the pilgrimage are accomplished. Near this wide and arid valley the *aḍḥā* takes place, the 'greater sacrifice' which is again a commemoration of Abraham who, in his total obedience to God's command, prepared to immolate his son (according to Islam this was Ishmael, not Isaac), for whom a ram was miraculously exchanged. The pilgrims celebrate this event by sacrificing thousands of sheep and distributing meat to the poor, while in every other land where Muslims are to be found, the same rite is observed, since this day, the tenth of the month of *Ḥajj*, is the greatest feast day (*ᶜĪd al-Aḍḥā*) in the Muslim calendar.

The other rites of the *ḥajj* take place in the immediate environs of the Holy City. At Minā, the pilgrims cast pebbles at three pillars which represent Satan, whom Abraham had repudiated when in this place.

This rapid description of the rites reveals that Abraham is a constant point of reference during the *Ḥajj*. It is, however, important to realise that the sacred places of Islam are also linked to the memory of Adam. A tradition relates that the first man and woman, being cast out from Paradise, were separated from each other and wandered through the earth, until God's grace allowed them to be reunited at ᶜArafa. It is also said that the first Kaᶜba was constructed by Adam and destroyed during the Flood, to be rebuilt later by Abraham, after which it was restored by Muhammad to the pure cult of monotheism which had been forgotten for many generations.

In this way the pilgrim to the Centre, which is represented on earth by Mecca, affirms not only his membership of the community of Muhammad, but also his attachment to the tradition of Abraham and, hence, that of Adam. At the place where the first human couple found grace once more in the sight of God, he is aware that he is cleansing himself of his sins, for the day of ᶜArafa is the day of forgiveness.

It is with a sense of regeneration at the wellspring of the universal Revelation that when the *ḥajj* proper is at an end he turns his steps to Medina to visit the grave of the Prophet, an act which is not obligatory but which is none the less observed by almost every pilgrim. When circumstances permit, a good number also go on to Jerusalem, the third Holy City of Islam, where they meditate in the Aqṣā Mosque near the sacred rock from which Muhammad was taken up through the seven heavens on the night of the *Miᶜrāj*, and where they pay their respects to the prophets of Israel, and to Jesus and his mother, who also were messengers of the eternal Truth.

Bearing henceforth the name of *ḥājj*, the pilgrim returns home endowed with new prestige. His village or district of town celebrates his return, for he has come back saturated with *baraka*, the benign spiritual influence which emanates from the Centre, and by which the descendants of Adam reconnect themselves to their timeless origin.

Developments in communication have brought about a huge increase in the number of pilgrims, especially since the Second World War. Their number, which is not easy to calculate, appears to vary between one and a half to two million, according to the most credible estimates. But to those who participate in the *Ḥajj*, or 'Greater Pilgrimage', which takes place annually in the lunar month of Dhu'l-Ḥijja, one may add those believers who, at other times of the year, make the *ᶜumra*, the Lesser Pilgrimage. Restricted to a visit to the *ḥaram* and to performing the rites connected with it, this is less meritorious, but still attracts a constant and substantial stream of devout visitors, who raise the number of pilgrims who visit Mecca in a single year to several millions.

This mass of pilgrims represents the whole Muslim world—in other words, practically every race on earth. Countries apparently secularised, or 'laicised', such as Turkey, are far from providing the smallest contingents, and this, together with the remarkable fervour of all present, forms another testimony to the extraordinary vitality with which Islam resists the current decline of the religions.

Although not a 'pillar' in the same way, the *jihād*, or 'holy war', which Muslims nowadays prefer to translate as 'collective effort', is usually included among the canonical obligations. In fact it represents a duty which bears some resemblance to the obligation imposed by modern states on their nationals in times of armed conflict, when each citizen is required to make his contribution to the national defense effort, and even to give his life for his country. The same sacrifice is traditionally required of the believer in the defence of Islam. None the less, for a *jihād* to be officially declared by the religious authorities, a number of conditions have to be met which nowadays are rarely present. It is therefore interpreted in a broader sense which covers every form of effort and struggle for the preservation and progress of religion. In this regard we may recall the *ḥadīth* according to which the Prophet, upon his return from a battle, defined warfare against external enemies as the 'lesser *jihād*', saying that the 'greater *jihād*' was that which the believer wages against his own ego.*

Circumcision (*khitān*) of male infants, a tradition of a particularly Abrahamic character, is a practice generally observed among all Muslim peoples, being regarded as necessary but not absolutely obligatory by the jurists. It is not laid down by the Qur'an,

* This *ḥadīth* is not included in the most authoritative anthologies of Prophetic traditions, and some writers have questioned its authenticity, or have ascribed it to one of the Prophet's Companions. Its importance to the spiritual life of long generations of Muslims has nonetheless been immense.

and is not an overriding necessity for those who convert to the faith.

The practice of Islam also includes a series of usages and prescriptions of varying degrees of importance, which, together with the 'pillars', leave their stamp on Muslim individual and collective life. Among the most important provisions one must firstly mention the prohibition of pork and of intoxicating drinks.

Westerners, even Orientalists, rarely see anything more in these prohibitions than their hygienic aspect. They have, however, a much more profound significance. Abstaining from the flesh of the pig, a dirty and vile animal which eats anything it can find, reminds the believer of the necessity of preserving himself, not simply on the level of food, but also from all that is impure in creation. It does have benefits for the health, but these are not what is essential.

As for the interdiction of alcohol, as also of other stimulants and narcotics, this reflects the requirement imposed on the believer, by reason of the five daily prayers, of being constantly able to address God without losing his self-mastery for an instant. Assuredly, poets such as Ibn al-Fāriḍ did sing of intoxication and of wine, but in an exclusively mystical sense, as the only wine permitted in Islam is that of Paradise.

It should be stated that these prohibitions are not possessed of an absolute character, and that here, as in every practice of Islam, the essential lies in the intention of the believer. The Qur'an is perfectly explicit on the subject:

> *God has only forbidden you carrion, blood, pig-flesh and animals over which the name of other than God has been recited. No sin attaches to those who are driven by necessity without being rebellious or transgressors. God is the All-Forgiving, the All-Merciful.* (11:173)

Another two prohibitions should be mentioned: one relating to the taking of interest on loans, which is regarded as usury (*ribā*), however low the rate, and the other which deals with games of chance (*maysir*), which the Qur'an calls 'the work of the devil'.

The ban on interest-taking has already been the subject of abundant commentaries by writers both ancient and modern, many of whom have seen fit to discount its moral and social aspects, and also the practical, economic advantages. We will confine ourselves here to noting once more that the traditional laws of Islam, the objectives of which are on an incomparably higher level than any idea of socio-economic 'progress' or 'development', serve to protect man from enslavement to the material and quantitative world. Moreover, it is undeniable that the impossibility of generating interest on loans reduces substantially the power of money. In other respects, in the present time, this traditional defence poses sizeable problems to Muslim countries which are closely tied to a world economic system which is not Islamic in origin. It would be an overstatement to claim that the solutions adopted have fully satisfied the requirements of Muslim orthodoxy. But however this may be, in a normative Islamic society still undisturbed by modern trends, the prohibition of *ribā*, combined with the obligation to pay the *zakāt*, is a positive factor which contributes to the equilibrium of economic life, which cannot contain its own ends, but must acquiesce in its place in the hierarchy of values which conform to the Islamic perspective.

As for gambling, which is manifestly opposed to the spirit of responsibility which Islam always seeks to inculcate, the prohibition was directed primarily at a custom prevalent among the pre-Islamic Arabs, who, before taking important decisions, would seek an augury by means of divining arrows. From this it was extended to all forms of gambling, including lotteries and betting on horses. As a form of sport, however, horseraces are not forbidden; in fact they are encouraged, since, according to a *ḥadīth*, the Prophet himself did not disdain to race with his companions.

Relations between the sexes and the role of women in the Muslim world have often been the subject of erroneous interpretations on the part of Westerners, particularly now that it is claimed that a total equality of the sexes has been established—something which, in any case, could not be attempted without betraying the vocation of the sexes in the cosmic order. In reality, however, it has been amply demonstrated that Islam considerably improved the lot of women in comparison with pre-Islamic societies, or even with the arrangements traditionally prevalent in Jewish and Christian communities, recognising new rights (such as the right of female inheritance) together with legal guarantees regarding their role as wives and mothers. It has also been remarked that it was not until the Napoleonic Code that equivalent rights were granted to women in the West. Yet the best characterisation of woman's role in Islam is supplied by the word 'dignity'. For it is this—in contrast to the degradation of women which has ensued from the modern obsession with sex—which has been assured to women in every truly Muslim society, in spite of the egotism of men and their frequent lack of observance (if not of the letter, than at least of the spirit) of the provisions of the faith.

This truth is not compromised by the fact that Islam recognises the principle of polygamy, and that every Muslim male may have up to four wives. The Qur'an, however, does not give this authorisation without a certain reserve:

> *Marry, of the women who seem good to you, two or three or four. But if you fear that you cannot treat them fairly, then one alone . . ..* (IV:3)
> *You will not be able to deal equally between women, however greatly you may wish it.* (IV:129)

This tolerance, which makes it understood that monogamy is fundamentally preferable, has given the traditional legislation enough flexibility to respond to the range of situations which may appear in human society, and, in its realism, has often been advantageous to women, who, in the Muslim world, have in general been able to integrate themselves into a family cell without either being abandoned or 'left on the shelf'. None the less, the sufficiently broad parameters which Islam has established may not be overstepped, and any relation between a man and woman outside the legal framework is considered as *zinā*, fornication: a blameworthy and punishable act.

With the same awareness of human nature, Islam traditionally permits divorce, even though a *ḥadīth* describes it as 'the most detestable to God of all permitted things'. On this point, as on others, Islam avoids burdening man with more than he can bear, and reserves its absolute demands, not for morality, which is by definition relative, but for the domain of faith.

The ensemble of traditional prescriptions which we have just outlined constitutes the *Sharīʿa*, the Law of divine inspiration, to which all who have accepted Islam must submit. It embraces all facets, and guides all activities, of life, which is thereby sacralised and brought into harmony with the Creator's will.

The interpretation of the *Sharīʿa* and its application in individual and collective existence form the subject of *fiqh*, which, like the non-juridical religious disciplines, draws its inspiration from four key sources: (a) the Qur'an, (b) the tradition (*sunna*) of the Prophet, as defined by the totality of *ḥadīths*, (c) deduction by analogy (*qiyās*) in cases not specifically covered by the Qur'an or the *Sunna*, and (d) the *ijmāʿ*, or consensus of the community of believers, which, according to the teachings of the Prophet, 'shall never agree on an error'.

Tradition teaches that solutions to every problem must be sought on the basis of these sources, with the help of *ijtihād*, 'personal effort'. The practice of this, none the less, is restricted to experts possessed of the requisite qualifications, since Islam does not know 'free examination' (as this exists in Protestant Christianity, for instance) and does not allow that men are capable of amending the Law to suit their convenience, or to conform with the tendencies of a given age. To underline the fact that the *Sharīʿa* exists in the definitive form which it must retain until the Day of Judgement, some theologians are of the opinion that the 'gate of *Ijtihād* is closed', and remain hostile to the attempts which modernists have made since the nineteenth century to reform the content and implementation of the Law by adapting it to changing times.

Following these principles, Muslim law constitutes an imposing and highly elaborate system which has left its mark on all the peoples of the *Umma*. It incorporates a number of juridical traditions which correspond to the major subdivisions within Islam, and to certain tendencies born during the first centuries of its history.

The Sunnis, who constitute more than four-fifths of the Muslim world community, are distributed for the most part into four juridical schools, or rites (*madhāhib*, sing. *madhhab*), each of which is regarded as legitimate by the other three. They were founded by the *imāms* Abū Ḥanīfa, Mālik, al-Shāfiʿī and Ibn Ḥanbal, who lived during the second and third centuries of the Hegira. These schools are distinguished from each other by slight variations of emphasis in the interpretation and application of the *Sharīʿa* rules, rather than by real divergences. All four are taught at the al-Azhar University at Cairo, which, although founded in ancient times by Shīʿites, has long been regarded as the citadel of Sunni orthodoxy.

The Shīʿites also follow schools of jurisprudence emanating from their own tradition, and in the elaboration of which the Imams played a determining role. The tiny but ancient Khārijite minority, of whom the Ibāḍīs constitute the most important group, apply a particularly literalist interpretation of the traditional Law.

On the whole, these various schools all teach the same *Sharīʿa*, each bringing into relief certain aspects which correspond to the differing tendencies and temperaments which have appeared through the centuries among the Muslim peoples. The most striking divergences between them largely concern questions of the outward form of the religious practices, together with the application of the law, taken in the restricted sense of the term. In the general domain of ethics, however, it is impossible to find differences of real significance, and one may therefore speak of Islamic morality as a body of precepts which are valid for all Muslims.

The ensemble of ethical regulations which proceed from the *Sharīʿa*, of which we have already had cause to mention many of the more important and characteristic, has for long centuries guaranteed the stability and harmony of Muslim society, providing it with both structure and coherence. All these prescriptions, which are not the product of social processes, but of God's command, create conditions favourable both to the accomplishment of the spiritual vocation of man, and to his flowering as an earthly creature. Neither have they lacked the dimension of realism by demanding the impossible or ignoring the frailty of human nature.

Moreover, in the observance of the Law, as in all other acts, Islam demands sincerity and rectitude before all else. A fundamental teaching of the Prophet, which appears at the beginning of most collections of *ḥadīth*, proclaims that 'actions are judged according to the intentions which lie behind them.'

This maxim is more than usually important at a time when the practice of the *Sharīʿa* poses problems which were unknown to former generations, being the product of a different general ambiance, and of certain tendencies which are subversive and hostile to every traditional Law and which the modern mind has thrown up everywhere. This is because even if believers are denied the opportunity of observing all the rules, their intention maintains their spirit, and this will be judged sufficient.

It must be properly recognised that throughout the Muslim world the *Sharīʿa* is not being followed as it was even one or two generations ago. It is increasingly rare to find a state which applies it comprehensively, and the majority of countries which still term themselves Muslim implement it in a piecemeal fashion, mixed with elements of law borrowed from the West.

On the personal and family level, the traditional ethic inspired by the *Sharīʿa* is facing a still greater challenge, particularly from a section of the younger generation which, in imitation of young people in Europe and America, has repudiated the old customs and finds it increasingly hard to accept discipline and authority of any kind. Morals regarding women, too, have changed, and there is a marked tendancy to refuse the norms and customs which, for fourteen hundred years—whatever current opinion and prejudice may claim—have assured their dignity and security in the Islamic context. Although much less virulent than the Western 'women's liberation' movement, this tendency can still assume the form of a rebellion against the traditional family structure which has preserved the stability of Muslim society for so long.

These trends have been favoured by the social and economic upheavals which have convulsed Muslim countries since the Second World War and imposed new models of life which are generally discordant with the Islamic tradition. It is undeniable, too, that the *Sharīʿa*, the norm of human life lived in conformity with God's will, is presently experiencing a decline the likes of which has not been seen down the centuries since the time of the Prophet. Of course, innumerable believers remain sincerely attached to it, but, in a world where a spirit of negation and revolt continues to gain ground, its practice requires more and more persistence and effort.

Those who have retained their loyalties will in any case not go unrewarded, since, according to a *ḥadīth* which speaks of the twilight which must inexorably spread over this earth: 'he who neglected a tenth part of Islam at its beginning shall be lost, whereas he that preserved a tenth part at the end shall win salvation.'

SOURCE TEXTS

True righteousness

Righteousness does not consist in turning your faces to East or West; but righteous is he that believes in God and the Last Day, and the Angels and the Scripture, and the Prophets; and gives his wealth, for love of Him, to kinsfolk and to orphans, and the needy and the wayfarer, and to those who ask; and sets slaves free, and observes the Prayer and pays the Alms-tax.

And those who keep their undertakings when they enter into them;

And those who are patient in adversity, suffering, and times of danger:

Such are the sincere. Such are the God-fearing.

Qur'an, II:177

Jesus and his mother according to the Qur'an

The Angels said: O Mary! God has chosen you, and made you pure, and has preferred you over all the women of creation. Qur'an, III:42

And when the Angels said: O Mary! God gives you glad tidings of a word from Him, whose name is the Messiah, Jesus son of Mary, illustrious in the world and in the hereafter, and one of those brought near [to Him].

He will speak unto mankind in his cradle, and in his manhood, and is of the righteous.

She said: My Lord! How might I have a child when no man has touched me? He said: So shall it be. God creates what He will. If He decrees a thing, He says unto it only Be! and it is. Qur'an, III:45–7

And [We chastised the Jews] because of their disbelief, and of their speaking against Mary a vile calumny,

And because of their saying, We killed the Messiah, Jesus son of Mary, God's messenger—yet they slew him not, nor crucified him, but it was made to appear so to them; and those who disagree concerning it are in doubt thereof; they have no knowledge of it save pursuit of a conjecture; they did not slay him for certain.

But God took him up to Himself. God is ever Mighty, Wise.

There is not one of the People of the Book but will believe in him before his death, and on the Day of Judgement he shall be a witness against them.

Qur'an, IV:156–9

O people of the Book! Be not extreme in your religion, nor say anything of God but the truth.

The Messiah, Jesus son of Mary, is but a prophet of God, and His word which He cast unto Mary, and a spirit from Him. Qur'an, IV:171

Whoever does the *Ḥajj* is never the same again

A *Ḥajji* should enter the *Ḥaram* for the first time by the *Bab as-Salam* (the door of Salvation). 'Lord, Thou art Salvation, and from Thee comes Salvation. We beg Thee, therefore, to receive us, grant us Thy salvation, and admit us to Paradise where Salvation is to be found.' Who is speaking? Are the words I hear coming from my own lips, or are they those that are being spoken at the same time by my unknown neighbour, by the thousands of people unknown to me, my brothers?

I do not have time to decide whether I have pronounced the ritual words or whether they have been spoken for me. The portal under which we were passing is already behind us. Beyond it, if I am correct, is the inner courtyard of the Temple. It is still dark, and being completely taken up by my invocations and by the spectacle of the crowd, I had seen little beyond the portal itself. But having passed it, I become aware that the others' progress and my own is slowing down, even stopping. I raise my eyes.

What I had not seen before, I see now. The simple, very simple, cube, draped in the simple, very simple black cloth, melts into the dimness of the dawn. It appears almost unreal, as if it were suspended rather than standing on the ground. The hallucinating round of worshippers look as if they are the plinth of the Kaʿba, bearing it aloft in triumph.

I find tears flowing down my cheeks. Coming from I know not where. I am no longer the same man. Not only am I no longer the disbelieving or indifferent person I had been at times, but I am no longer even the abstract believer that I was formerly, only a few instants ago. That believer who was so anxious to understand and to analyse, both others and himself, to put himself, his every gesture in perspective—with perhaps, at the back of his mind, that he would later want to find the right words to describe all this, to explain it to intellectuals like himself; that philosopher-believer, I no longer know him, I no longer recognise myself in him.

No, I am now merely a man with tears running down his face. Fortunately, the words that I am required to recite are simple, so simple, saying precisely the only things that I want to cry out at this moment: 'God is great! God is great! There is no other god but God!' And my tears flow and flow. I say my prayers in two *rak'as* with my face bathed in tears. Literally flooded. And I feel as if I had been bathed within, flooded within.

Ezzedine Guellouz, *Pilgrimage to Mecca*

6

Civilisation of oneness

WHEN they burst forth from the desert carrying the message which would transform the existence of so many peoples, the first Muslims were hardly what would today be called 'civilised.' Apart from the ideas and traditions which allowed them to survive in the hostile environment of the vast Arabian spaces, all the knowledge available to these simple and unpolished people was contained in the revealed Book and the teachings of the Prophet who had just departed from their midst. In the realm of art they possessed nothing more than a few crafts, which gave them weapons and the necessary adjuncts to their pastoral way of life, while their literature was confined to the poems and epics with which the Bedouins accompanied their festivals and their interminable wanderings on camelback. All this was not devoid of a certain vigorous beauty, but, according to our modern criteria, we may still characterise as 'primitive' the Arabs who, in the middle of the seventh century, set forth to conquer the world.

A few decades on, after the installation of their Caliphate at Damascus, these same rough and 'primitive' Arabs had laid the foundations for a new civilisation which was to prove one of the most refined and brilliant of all time. Drawing on a vast diversity of sources and material, it revealed an extraordinary assimilative power which allowed it, throughout the centuries and in all the regions in which it took root, to retain a remarkable degree of coherence and homogeneity, and to remain, like everything else which emanates from Islam, centred on the principle of oneness.

It is impossible to fathom the true nature of this civilisation, or to understand how it differed fundamentally from the post-Renaissance civilisation of Europe, without understanding the major principles which it enshrined, and which continued to inspire it for as long as it remained authentically Muslim. It must be stated first of all that it was a genuine expression of Islam as such; that is to say, that in all its modes it evinced an attitude of submission and conformity to the Divine Will.

The world view of Islamic culture has always flowed directly from revelation, and hence from transcendent and eternal truths rather than from speculations or 'systems' elaborated by philosophers or other thinkers. From the numerous legacies available to it from earlier or foreign cultures it borrowed only to the extent that these accorded with its own perspective, and could be 'Islamised' in a thoroughgoing way.

If one defines the 'sacred' as the traces of the Absolute in the relative, of the Infinite in the finite, or of the Intemporal in the timebound, then the civilisation of Islam must be characterised as sacred. It has always retained its consciousness of, and witness to, the higher realities whose reflections it projects onto this lower world. Its fundamental attitude has always been, in one way or another, an implementation of the first *Shahāda: Lā ilāha illa-'Llāh*, 'there is no deity but God'—since it has always evoked the divine without deifying creation, in contrast to modern (and particularly scientific) thought, which perceives a consistent reality only in the created order, in which it delineates the nature of the absolute in a highly abusive fashion.

In all the domains and activities which together form what we call 'civilisation', the Muslims have constantly retained a recollection of the metaphysical reality expressed so perfectly by the *Shahāda*. At the end of the day, it is this remembrance alone which confers real value on every human activity. For according to a *ḥadīth*, God has cursed everything in this lower world, with the sole exception of the recollection (*dhikr*) of His name. A

Muslim undertakes nothing, particularly in the domain of knowledge and the arts, without having previously uttered the invocation 'In God's name': *bismillāh*.

Suffused by a sense of the divine, Islamic civilisation has always embodied a wisdom which has preserved it from excess. Although it does not deify the cosmos, as modern man has done, it discerns perfectly its symbolic character, which transmutes it into an expression of higher realities. In consequence, it respects it and exists in harmony with it. By way of contrast, it is a striking fact that the present, Promethean civilisation confers, on the one hand, an absolute value on the created world, and on the other—no longer knowing how to read the 'signs' of God therein—desacralises it, and finishes by destroying its equilibrium, with all the far-reaching consequences—most strikingly for the environment—which this has entailed.

Muslim philosophers, scholars and artists, however, have never secularised the universe. Being aware of the universal laws which regulate every level of existence, they submit to them without pretending to innovate constantly, or to 'progress' indefinitely in the finite realms of nature. They regard the created order through a synthetic perspective which assigns each thing to its place in a universal hierarchy. The Muslim of the classical period thus lived in a world which was entirely coherent, in which everything was endowed with meaning, and which did not merely contribute to creating a balanced and harmonious atmosphere, but also reminded him ceaselessly of its ultimate goals.

The civilisation of Islam also possessed the power to transmute the milieu in which it spread and flourished, creating therein conditions of life which might appear enviable to many of our contemporaries, even those who live in the most 'developed' countries; but even beyond this, it imprinted its own 'spiritual style' upon it, a sacred ambience which gave profound sense to the lives of all. In this environment, even the most modest strata of the population enjoyed access to many benefits which enhanced their material existence, while still resembling travellers passing through a world in which they established no fixed abode, since they knew themselves destined for another, less transient world.

Of course, Islam, unlike modern socialist theories, has never claimed to establish any sort of 'paradise on earth', since it teaches that the Hereafter is preferable to the present world, and that men, by using the blessings granted them by God, must seek the 'final abode' before all else. Muslim civilisation, therefore, has never represented a state of perfection, and, side by side with its splendour, has not been free from defects and a variety of evils, including situations which the modern mind would interpret as social injustices. However, it is at least realistic, and, in contrast to the modern utopias, their fantasies and their chimera, has never pursued the unattainable. Of course, it is not lacking in a certain idealism, if we understand by this term the principles which we have just outlined; but, knowing what man is in the wholeness of his being, it takes account of his weaknesses while attempting to mitigate their effects, and at the same time offers him the best possible opportunities—taking cosmic conditions into account—of realising his primary vocation, which grooms him for immortality.

An interesting example of this kind of 'realism allied to the highest principles' is provided by slavery, despite the false or tendentious interpretations to which it has often been subjected. Islamic civilisation has traditionally practiced a form of slavery regulated by the *Sharīʿa*. Although this softens its rigours and subjects it to restrictions unknown to earlier societies, one is often asked why Islam did not go one step further by simply decreeing its abolition.

To answer this question, it should first be remarked that Islam has tolerated slavery but has never approved of it, and that all its teachings and prescriptions in this regard lead to its alleviation as far as possible in the short term, and, in the longer term, conduce to its progressive suppression. To abolish it would have been impossible in a world in which it was generally practiced by all the states which bordered on the new Muslim empire, and in which the idea of challenging the principle itself had not occurred to anyone. It was the custom to enslave prisoners of war—when these were not simply massacred—and the Islamic state would have put itself at a grave disadvantage vis-à-vis its enemies had it not reciprocated to some extent. By guaranteeing them humane treatment, and various possibilities of subsequently releasing themselves, it ensured that a good number of combatants in the opposing armies preferred captivity at the hands of Muslims to death on the field of battle.

It should be very clearly underlined that the slavery once practiced in the Muslim world cannot be compared to the form it had assumed—for instance—in the Roman Empire. Islamic legislation subjected slaveowners to a set of precise obligations, first among which was the slave's right to life, for, according to a *ḥadīth*, 'Whoever kills his slave shall be killed by us'. In consequence, the murder of a slave was punished like that of a free man.

There are many other *ḥadīths* which define Islam's true attitude in this regard. The Prophet said: 'Your slaves are your brethren; therefore whoever has a brother who depends upon him must feed and clothe him in the way he feeds and clothes himself; and should not impose upon him tasks which exceed his capacity; should you ask them to do such things, then you are obliged to help them.' The *Sharīʿa* takes this injunction, among many others, into account when defining the responsibilities and duties of slaveholders.

There is another teaching which enjoins respect for the human dignity of slaves: 'Let none of you say, "This man, or this woman, is my slave". He must rather say: "This is my man, and this my woman."' Putting into relief the provisional character of social ties and the authority exercised by slaveowners over their slaves, the Prophet said: 'It is true that God has made you their masters, but, had He so wished, He could equally well have made you their slaves.'

To manumit a slave has always been regarded as one of the most meritorious of all acts, and many passages of the Qur'an recommend or even require it, particularly as a means of expiation for serious faults. Traditional legislation lays down the methods of voluntary liberation of slaves by their masters (*ᶜitq*), and there were very many Muslims who observed these, especially at the end of their lives, so as not to die and appear before God without having given full freedom to the human beings placed in their power during their earthly lives.

Additionally, slaves had the ability to enfranchise themselves at their own initiative, without waiting passively for the goodwill of their masters: the procedure known as *mukātaba* allowed them to buy their own freedom with sums which they saved from their work, and which the state frequently augmented with advances—a measure which the slaveowner had no right to oppose. In contrast to the situation under Roman law, slaves were not deprived of the legal ability to exercise their rights and to appeal to a judge against their masters in all cases of illegal treatment.

Besides domestic slavery, which was generally imbued with a patriarchal character, there also existed a form of military slavery, which was frequently employed by princes in need of recruits, especially for their personal guards. This situation had the effect of conferring an often considerable influence and power on men of servile condition or origin, and some of these became the founders of great and illustrious dynasties, such as the Tulunids and Mamlukes of Egypt.

The object of a prosperous commercial sector, which under the Abbasid Empire was often the speciality of non-Muslims, particularly Byzantine and Venetian Christians, and Jews, slavery gradually declined in importance until, at the beginning of the present century, it was confined to a few survivals which have now disappeared entirely. Thanks to the strict traditional controls which have always regulated the practice, it would be difficult to deny that social conditions were remarkably humane during the great periods of Muslim civilisation, and that these, moreover, were in conformity with the 'egalitarian' spirit of Islam, which, in a *ḥadīth*, teaches that 'the blackest of Abyssinians' is superior to the most noble of Quraishites, if he has more faith.

To understand how the spirit of Islam truly expresses itself in a civilisation, one must understand the essential function of its art, which shapes the forms which make up the context of the life of the believing community, and thus creates the most suitable environment for each man's earthly journey and return to God. In this regard, Muslim art is a 'sacred art' in the fullest sense of the term.

It is significant that in Islamic civilisation the development of the plastic arts preceded that of literature and the sciences, precisely because their role is more basic to the practice of the religion. For they express sacred doctrine and metaphysical truth in a way which is more direct and existential than literature, philosophy or the sciences, the modes of which are discursive in nature.

The Umayyad caliphate (AD 661–750) was the era of development in which Muslim art laid down the main lines of its special aesthetic and defined its spiritual and social functions. Its first achievements were mostly the work of Christian (or recently converted) artists and architects, which is why they incorporate so many survivals of earlier aesthetic concepts, the majority of which were Byzantine. This is particularly evident in the magnificent palaces of the Umayyad rulers in Syria, which abound in representations of human and animal figures in an manner foreign to the later style of Islam. None the less, side by side with this worldly and profane art, these same caliphs constructed two great monuments which mark the first stage of typically Muslim sacred art: the Dome of the Rock at Jerusalem, and the Umayyad Mosque at Damascus.

Wrongly styled the 'Mosque of Omar' by Europeans, the

Dome of the Rock, which stands over the sacred rock of the ancient Temple of Solomon, and from which the Prophet was carried up to heaven on the night of the *Miʿrāj*, is still in a typically Byzantine style, although it is already Muslim property in virtue of its spirit and the serene harmony of its lines. Being more a focus of pilgrimage and a place of meditation than a building destined for congregational worship, it could hardly have served as a model for mosque-builders, although its famous dome did exercise some degree of influence over the Muslim architects.

The Great Mosque of Damascus, which occupies the site of an ancient Greek temple which was later transformed into a church dedicated to St John the Baptist ('Yaḥyā' to Muslims), was built at the start of the eighth century by the caliph al-Walīd, who, recycling the materials of the old building, reproduced the layout of the first mosque of the Prophet at Medina. This gave it special importance in the evolution of Muslim sacred architecture, notably in connection with its articulation of spaces destined for collective prayer.

A decorative component of these two monuments should be noted: both contain magnificent mosaics which still gain the admiration of visitors. These incorporate a wide variety of plant motifs, and, especially at Damascus, depict landscapes with imaginary towns and palaces. Nothing, however, appears to be living, whether human or animal, in conformity with a prohibition which—for places of worship—has always been strictly observed since the dawn of Islam.

More interestingly still, the decoration of these two famous buildings remains wholly unique in the history of Muslim art, for after their construction a complete ban on figurative representation was maintained, with the exception of some stylised plant motifs used for arabesques. Even these were only permitted when juxtaposed with inscriptions from the Qur'an; and the rejection of images, often termed 'aniconism', became a major characteristic of Islamic art.

This ban, however, has never been absolute; and tradition has often in practice tolerated dimensionless images quite freely, although only in the context of secular arts not directly linked into religious practice. As a general rule, this tolerance has not extended to images which 'project a shadow', and hence to statuary, which, with a handful of noteworthy exceptions such as the famous Court of the Lions at Granada's Alhambra Palace, has been absent from Muslim civilisation.

Human representation found its most attractive and abundant expression in the painting of miniatures, an art form in which Persian artists have particularly excelled—although some Arabs, Turks and Indians have also showed great talent. These artists left superb masterpieces which, although unquestionably forming part of the artistic patrimony of Muslim civilisation, none the less do not authentically express its own special genius. For even though it has legimitised itself by submitting to strict rules—such as a prohibition on perspective and relief—the miniature is still, when compared to typically Islamic arts such as the arabesque or calligraphy, of a somewhat marginal and exceptional character. It is also significant that it has always been regarded as doubtful or even inadmissible by a number of religious authorities.

What must be highlighted is that since the time of its earliest expressions, Muslim art displayed an originality and a genius which distinguished it immediately and in the most radical fashion from all that had gone before. The newness of the Revelation had manifested itself also in the forms which would help to create the unique atmosphere of Islam.

Modern orientalists and art critics have produced some weighty studies and commentaries on the questions relating to the elaboration of Muslim art, often coming up with facts of real historical or documentary interest. They have also expressed, however—and taught in their universities—a distorted understanding of this art and its function within the traditional framework of Islamic civilisation, usually as a result of their inadequate grasp of the vast gulf which divides it from post-Renaissance modernity. This function has never been of an aesthetic or 'cultural' order, in the current sense of these words, and, unlike modern Western art, it has never functioned as a means of expression for individual personalities. For the basic theme of all genuinely Muslim art is the One, and Its manifestation in multiplicity; and no artist can conform to this without his individuality being effaced.

In this connection reference should be made to a very characteristic confusion made by some authors concerning the notion of 'abstract art', which, it is believed, may be applied similarly, and in the same sense, both to traditional Islam's refusal to imitate palpable appearances and to the non-figurative art of the modern West. In reality, apart from a few superficial and accidental similarities, these two forms of 'abstract art' have nothing in common, their motivations being diametrically opposed.

On the one hand, Muslim 'abstract art' proceeds in its unique way from the *Shahāda*, which is a denunciation of the 'cosmic illusion', and forbids man to project one order of reality onto another (or the nature of the Absolute into the relative); all to enable him to discern and celebrate the signs of oneness in multiplicity. By contrast, most productions of non-figurative modern art reveal the dissolution of a reality which has been severed from its metaphysical referents and has hence become unable to exist by itself; in consequence, it has primarily become a means of expressing the unconscious and its irrational turbulences.

The theme of the One, which sustains every artistic production which is truly Muslim, is particularly explicit in the decorative art of mosques, in which the two principal modes are the arabesque and Qur'anic inscriptions. Their combination engenders an atmosphere of serenity which is eminently conducive to prayer and meditation: the best possible milieu for the flourishing of Islamic piety and spirituality.

From the legacies of ornament handed down from earlier

civilisations, the arabesque retained no more than two fundamental elements: interlacing patterns and plant motifs, these latter being so stylised as to make it hard to discern the exact botanic species to which the constituents belong. It deploys two essential characteristics of Muslim art: geometric genius, and a sense of rhythm which is nomadic in origin. The beauty thus created has been described as 'Platonic' by some modern writers, since it locates itself on the universal plane of 'ideas' and 'forms'. And indeed, it contains nothing that is individualistic or passional, its quality being more 'metaphysical' than 'mystical', since it affirms ceaselessly the transcendence of God.

Being a monumental articulation of the great Muslim art of calligraphy, the Qur'anic inscriptions found in mosques and other religious buildings such as mausolea are certainly meant to be read and understood; but one may paradoxically state that this does not necessarily comprise their prime function. They assure the recollection and presence of God's Word, and their beauty is on the whole more important than their intelligibility. This is why they are so regularly executed in the Kufic script: archaic and hard to decipher, yet majestic and hieratic. Moreover the letters are juxtaposed with the arabesques, so that together they help to create the sacred ambience of these buildings, which seem suffused by a divine incantation breathed into their very substance.

The most frequent inscription is obviously the divine Name, *Allāh*. This represents a visual form of *dhikr*, the 'remembrance' of God and the invocation of His name, to which many practices of Muslim piety lead, following numerous injunctions of the Qur'an, particularly the verse which runs: *Remember Me, and I shall remember you* [11:152].

This decorative art flourishes in innumerable mosques raised in styles which vary greatly according to the countries in which they are found and the national geniuses whose influence they express; but in which one everywhere finds the same atmosphere of serenity, which seems like a reflection of the bliss of Heaven.

Some of these are the pride of capitals such as Istanbul and Cairo, or of other cities which have played a major role in the history of Islam, such as Qayrawan, Tlemçen, Marrakech, Isfahan and Lahore, and also Cordova, whose mosque, although converted into a cathedral after the Christian conquest, none the less remains one of the purest masterpieces of Muslim architecture. These famous buildings, like many others which are more modest in scale and renown, manifest the limpid and objective quality of Muslim piety which has nothing dramatic or tormented about it, but for which beauty is simply an aspect of truth. For, according to a *ḥadīth* dear to artists, 'God is beautiful, and He loves beauty'.

Calligraphy, often combined with illumination, has always occupied a privileged position among the Islamic arts, of which it is among the most meritorious, since it primarily involves the reproduction of the sacred Book which is the inimitable expression of divine truth and wisdom. Great artists have excelled in this field, and names such as Ibn al-Bawwāb (early eleventh century AD) and Yāqūt al-Mustaᶜṣimī (end of the thirteenth century), are still celebrated, even though they are unlikely to have practiced their art to achieve fame in this world. The rare Qur'ans by their hand which survive today are among the most precious treasures of Muslim civilisation. The sacramental value which they represent necessarily escapes non-Muslims, although a pure and inexpressible beauty may shine from them to which they may respond. The exhibition of Qur'anic manuscripts organised during the Festival of Islam held in 1976 at London made a deep impression on Western visitors, and one critic from the newspaper *Le Monde* celebrated their mysterious splendour in an article bearing the wholly adequate title 'The Message of the Absolute'.

Qur'anic recitation, the oral equivalent of calligraphy, is a complex and subtle art as well as an essential liturgical act, since it causes the Divine Word to resonate in the ears of the believers. It has sometimes been the sole form of vocal or even musical art recognised by the religious authorities, because a number of theologians and doctors of the Law have felt a systematic mistrust of music and its ability to unleash the passional aspects of the human soul.

None the less, a universal civilisation such as Islam could not have ignored music. On the contrary, it allowed it to flourish, and to evolve into distinct schools and styles which reflected the diverse temperaments of the Muslim peoples. The memory of great musicians such as Isḥāq al-Mawṣilī of Baghdad, or his pupil Ziryāb, who made a career for himself at the court of the caliph of Cordova, has survived down to the present day. Music also formed the subject of highly learned theoretical works, the best known of which was the *Great Book of Music* of the renowned Abbasid philosopher al-Fārābī. Moreover, in this area the Christian Middle Ages were deeply influenced by the Muslims, a fact which has been established by the discoveries of musicologists and is reflected in the Arab etymology of the names of instruments such as the lute, the rebec and the guitar.

Modern listeners are in general unaware of the enormous richness of this art, being unable to apprehend its subtlety and refinement. It is as well to note here that despite the doubt and reserve felt by the most strict theologians, the traditional music cultivated in the Muslim lands is an authentically Muslim art capable not only of bringing about the most exalted aesthetic pleasure, but, by virtue of a structure and symbolism which transform it into a kind of audible arabesque, of elevating and calming the soul, and fixing it on the recollection of the One.

Like other traditional civilisations, Islam has never recognised a real distinction between art and the crafts. Objects in daily use are also works of art imbued with an aura of beauty which enriches the lives of all—or at least this was the case before the invasion of the fruits of modern industry. A characteristic instance is provided by carpets and ceramics, whose decorative and always 'abstract' ornamental motifs evince the same sense of rhythm and geometric genius which we find in arabesques. Products of these crafts, which always conform to norms and models handed down from generation to generation, show an aesthetic of which one never wearies, and which is innocent of all lapses in taste. They radiate a 'quality of life' which the products of the most 'developed' modern societies are often wholly unable to equal.

The above few pages have done no more than skim the surface of the vast field of Muslim art, and are mainly intended to show the spirit in which it should be approached. They should also serve to resolve a permanently latent confusion: art produced by Muslims is not necessarily Muslim art. It is becoming increasingly common to see people of Muslim origin seeking means of expression in art forms of modern Western inspiration which have nothing in common with the perspective and spiritual vision of Islam, even when their productions still—as they sometimes do—address subjects borrowed from 'Oriental life'. It is not enough to paint minarets, veiled women or even people at prayer to be 'doing' Islamic art, which, to be authentic, must express a quality of being which rises above the individual, and is linked, in the final analysis, to revelation. Anything else is simply folklore.

The sciences have constituted an even wider and more varied domain in the Muslim world than that of the arts, although the two are linked by close ties. As heirs to a patrimony of disciplines originating in the furthest antiquity, and later cultivated and developed by several Western and Oriental civilisations, the Islamic sciences represented the latest point in a great 'traditional' current, forming a coherent ensemble in which man could find answers to all the questions which he might ask himself about the created universe around him, and which also set sufficient practical and 'technical' means at his disposal to save him from being overcome by material preoccupations, thus enabling him to lead an existence worthy of his vocation as God's vicegerent on earth.

The sources of Islamic science are thus multiple, although three have been of central importance: pre-Islamic Persia, classical India, and Hellenic and hellenistic antiquity. The transmission of knowledge from the first two of these was relatively direct, thanks to the contacts which Muslims made with living representatives of these cultures following the conquest of the Near and Middle East. The intellectual heritage of Greece and Alexandria came to the Islamic world mainly through a massive and remarkable effort of translation which was carried out during the first two centuries of the Abbasid period. This activity was actively encouraged by the Baghdad caliphs, one of whom, al-Ma'mūn, founded in 830 the famous *Bayt al-Ḥikma*, the 'House of Wisdom', where the knowledge acquired from ancient sources was cultivated and extended, and the influence of which radiated through and even beyond the Muslim empire.

In this way the old sciences were infused into the new civilisation, where the names of Plato, Aristotle, Hippocrates, Galen, Euclid, and many others soon became familiar to every cultivated person. Nevertheless, only those writers were admitted whose works were judged to be compatible with the truths of the faith. In this respect a privileged place was reserved for Plato, sometimes looked upon as an equal to the Prophets, and whose name was not infrequently borne by Muslims themselves.

Modern historians and scholars regularly highlight the range of remarkable contributions made by Arab-Islamic civilisation to human science and knowledge in general. During its greatest ages, the Muslims demonstrated an insatiable intellectual curiosity, which was favoured by a liberty subject to hardly any brakes from the religious authorities, since the Prophet himself had actively recommended the search for knowledge, 'though it be in China'. And had he not taught also that the ink of scholars would be judged more precious than the blood of martyrs?

Christians, Jews, even Zoroastrians, participated actively in the intellectual life of the Muslim empire, notably as translators and transmitters of pre-Islamic texts, and their role in the elaboration of Arab medicine was a dominant one. All, however, brought their thinking into line with a metaphysic and cosmology which accorded with the teachings of the Qur'an and *Ḥadīth*. In such a context, whose legitimacy no-one even thought of challenging, the philosophers and scholars of the Muslim world considerably enlarged and enriched the field of human knowledge, making it both more exact and more capable of responding to the questions posed by the universe of natural phenomena.

It is essential to grasp that Islamic science was not divided into separate and more or less independant fields like modern science, but joined all of its branches into an organic unity. Scholars, refusing to be confined to one speciality, generally practiced several. The case of the great Avicenna (Ibn Sīnā), who was simultaneously a physician, mathematician, physicist, chemist, astronomer, philosopher, and even poet—not to mention his political activity—is particularly well-known, but there are many others who could also be cited. For instance, readers of the famous *Rubāʿiyyāt*, the quatrains of Omar Khayyam, are often unaware that their author, as well as being a poet, was a noted astronomer and mathematician.

In contrast to their modern colleagues, who have given themselves up to studies of a mainly analytic, quantitative and piecemeal nature, the scholars of classical Islam cultivated a more synthetic and qualitative science which reflected their more universal vision of the created world. They were thus able to incorporate the element of wisdom into their knowledge, which saved them from any attribution of absolute authority to science (which would be tantamount to deifying it), lest it slip from their control and turn against them.

Astronomy was always especially honoured by Islamic civilisation, in accordance with the Qur'an, which contains many passages encouraging man to contemplate the heaven and the earth, which contain the 'signs' of God. The Muslims therefore took to scrutinising the firmament meticulously, standing on hills or minarets to do so. History preserves the memory of the ninth-century Andalusian physician and astronomer ʿAbbās ibn Firnās, who used to sit on the hills around Cordova to study the movements of the stars, and who remains especially famous as the inventor of a flying machine, a glider made of feathers and cloth which allowed him to remain airborne for considerable periods —until the day came when it crashed.

Many other eminent men of science dedicated themselves to astronomy, supported by some of the caliphs of Baghdad and Cordova, followed by a whole line of rulers and princes up to the dawn of modern times, many of whom were patrons of observatories which were established in the major regions of the Islamic world. One of the most famous of these was at Marāgha in Persia, founded in the thirteenth century by the great savant Naṣīr al-Dīn Ṭūsī as a scientific institution of an almost modern character, which employed teams of researchers, many of whom had come from far-off countries.

Muslim astronomy boasted other great names (al-Farghānī, Thābit ibn Qurra, ʿAlī ibn Yūnus, al-Baṭṭānī, al-Bīrūnī, Shīrāzī, Kāshānī, to name only a few), and achieved enormous advances over the sciences of the ancients. It made many discoveries which were of critical importance in the history of human thought; for instance, it corrected many errors of Ptolemy's cosmology, it calculated the distance between earth and moon with an accuracy which is remarkable given the technical means available at the time; it discovered the third eccentricity of the moon, it discovered sunspots, and developed or perfected a vast array of scientific instruments, including the astrolabe and the azimuthal quadrant. It is interesting to note that although al-Bīrūnī developed, five centuries before Copernicus, a theory of the earth's rotation around the sun, this did not arouse the hostile reactions which it would one day provoke in Europe.

Historians of science have pointed out that without the assistance of the Muslim sciences, the savants of Europe would have been unable to elaborate the new astronomical and cosmological ideas which overturned the traditional vision of the universe and formed the basis for the ideas of modernity. One may, therefore, wonder why the scientific revolution never happened in the Islamic world. To this question, which is regularly posed by many philosophers, a modern Muslim scholar who is well versed in the sciences of both East and West has given the following response, which seems deeper than any earlier attempt to address it: 'The Muslims had all the technical knowledge necessary to overthrow the Ptolemaic system, including knowledge of the heliocentric system, but they did not do so because they had not as yet become forgetful of the symbolic content of traditional astronomy nor of the fact that the best way to remind most men of the presence of God is to remind them of the limited character of the created world.'*

Mathematics, a discipline which is closely linked to astronomy, also occupied a privileged position among the scientific disciplines of Muslim civilisation, where it developed considerably. A few facts should be enough to emphasise the breadth and scope of this impulse.

It was the Islamic world which, having borrowed them from India, popularised the use of the so-called 'Arabic' numerals, which it then passed on to Christendom. It was Muslim scholars, too, who developed decimal fractions and the function of the 'zero', a word which is itself of Arabic origin.† The name of one scholar, al-Khwārizmī, the first director of the House of Wisdom in Baghdad, should be especially remembered, as he is often included among the greatest geniuses of mankind. His work has even left profound influences on modern scientific terminology: it is to him that we owe the word 'algebra' (*al-jabr*), and 'algorithm' (through a corruption of his name into 'Alkarizmi').

* Seyyed Hossein Nasr, *Islamic Science*, London 1976.

† The Arabic for 'zero' is *ṣifr*, which has also given us the word 'cypher'; 'zero' coming via the Italian 'zefero'.

Overall, inestimable progress was made in the various branches of mathematics. As well as the invention of algebra, which they also applied to geometry, one might also mention—among a whole mass of examples—the fact that the Muslims were the true fathers of trigonometry, which allowed them to open the way to the discovery of logarithms and the resolution of an important body of problems, thanks to improvements which they made to methods of calculation.

Mathematics, despite their apparently quantitative character, in Islam never lost a certain qualitative content associated with Pythagoreanism. Muslims recognised the symbolic value of numbers, each of which proceeded from the most fundamental of all: the One, the origin of all things and the final destination to which they must all return. Mathematics was not, therefore, an exclusively profane science; instead it participated in the sacredness which impregnated all of Muslim civilisation, conferring upon it the sense of equilibrium and proportion which has always been its hallmark, particularly in its artistic expressions.

Muslims also made major contributions to man's knowledge of nature and his terrestrial environment, notably in the fields of botany and zoology. They can fairly be considered the real founders of physics and chemistry: even the name of the latter science is of Arabic origin.

It was probably the field of medicine, however, which more than any other discipline established the reputation of Arab-Islamic science in the West. In this regard it is interesting to note that the greatest scholars of Islam were also master-physicians as well. Ibn Sīnā (Avicenna) was the most famous, although many others could also be cited, such as al-Fārābī, Ibn Rushd (Averroes), al-Bīrūnī and al-Kindī.

The status thus enjoyed by medicine among the sciences was a reflection of the fact that it was not simply a system of curing, as it has become today, but was also a philosophy of man which flowed from a doctrine of humanity which accorded with the facts of Revelation and traditional cosmology. According to this perspective, the human being is a microcosm corresponding to the macrocosm, and summarises the totality of existence;* so that to know him opens a door to understanding the universe. Far from being a profane science confined to the bodily domain and aiming for exclusively palpable results, it is instead a form of wisdom which is integrated into the intellectual hierarchy of Islam and draws its inspiration from its message, as is shown by the title *ḥakīm* ('sage') which has often been conferred on physicians.

The Muslims drew extensively on those Greek medical sources which were compatible with their own perspective, but augmented these with extensive original research. Islamic medicine was taught until the end of the eighteenth century in the universities of Europe, where no-one was ignorant of the names of Avicenna (Ibn Sīnā), dubbed the 'Prince of Physic', whose *Canon*, a treatise on physiology, hygiene, pathology and therapeutics, ran through numerous Latin editions. Rhazes (Abū Bakr ibn Zakarīyā al-Rāzī) was also famous as the author of the first descriptions of diseases such as smallpox and measles, and also of the first work on pediatrics. Another name should also be cited: that of Ibn al-Nafīs, who, three centuries before Michael Servetus, discovered the lesser circulation of the blood.

Surgery, which was capable of performing complex operations such as those for cataracts, made use of methods unknown in the West until the last century, such as anaesthesia, which was brought about by various narcotics, and antiseptics, in which alcohol was the main ingredient. Most towns of any importance had their own hospital, where care was usually provided free of charge. Medicines, the range of which was considerably enlarged, were usually 'organic', and drew on a deep knowledge of the plant world.

The Muslim lifestyle was significantly influenced by medicine,

* According to an Arab maxim, 'man is the universe writ small, and the universe a man writ large.'

which, in conformity with the prescriptions of the *Sharīʿa*, applied a series of extremely sane rules of hygiene in matters relating to food and personal cleanliness. These rules encouraged the establishment of public and private baths everywhere, which, as well as being used for the ritual ablutions, were destined for therapeutic purposes, and often employed specialised masseurs.

So how much remains today of this great civilisation, so balanced, harmonious and refined, which, in addition to acknowledging the beauty of this world, offered man every opportunity to realise fully his transcendent vocation? Some very beautiful relics, to be sure, and some glorious survivals, but also many regrets.

The Islamic peoples, who look over their shoulders to the time when they were leaders of all nations, and who retain a sense of nostalgia for their erstwhile splendour, are bitterly conscious of their decline. The political and military supremacy of the West has humiliated them, and the progressive invasion of its industrial products, its customs, and, to a large extent, its ways of thought, have all provoked a deep disequilibrium in outlooks and patterns of life moulded by centuries of homogeneous tradition. What has happened is, so to speak, an 'alienation', which has belittled the specific, Islamically-based values, of these peoples, and imposed on them new values shipped in from abroad.

Set beside the dynamism which Europe has shown in every sphere since the sixteenth century, the immobility of the world of Islam generally appears as a deplorable and fatal decadence. Nevertheless, there exists a frequent tendency to exaggerate the sterility of later Muslim culture, and to belittle the numerous and often impressive artistic productions which date from the last four centuries. Some of the finest mosques of Islam, such as those built by Sinan in Turkey, or the Shah Mosque at Isfahan, date from the sixteenth and seventeenth centuries, and one of the greatest architectural masterpieces of all time, the Taj Mahal at Agra, was built by a Muslim ruler at the beginning of the reign of Louis XIV.

Similarly, the brilliance of Moghul culture was far from defunct when India fell under Western domination.

In most of the other Islamic lands, too, the traditional arts showed much vitality. But genuinely intellectual life seemed to be moribund, and the great Muslim universities such as al-Azhar at Cairo, the Qarawiyyīn at Fez, and the Zaytūna at Tunis, endlessly reiterated an ancient body of knowledge without attempting to renew it.

In any event, it must be stressed that this civilisation, however somnolent and inert it may have been, did at least remain faithful to Islam and perpetuate its essential values. It had, doubtlessly, lost the keys to earthly power, but it retained those of Heaven, and in the final analysis it is clearly this that matters. The West, for its part, followed the opposite road, and set out to conquer the world, at the risk—despite the warning of Christ—of losing its soul. But however this may be, the material impotence of the Muslim peoples was sooner or later bound to leave them effectively defenseless against an aggressive Western modernity, which was bound by its very nature to strike at the fundamental principles of Islam.

In spite of this, most Muslims today, alert mostly to the exterior aspect of things, feel a bitter resentment at having been 'overtaken' and left in a position of 'backwardness' relative to the modern West. They often ask themselves why the new dawn of 'progress' should have arisen in Christian Europe rather than in the Muslim world. The question is made more acute by the fact that the Muslims, at the close of the Middle Ages, had at their disposal all the elements of knowledge which would have enabled them to inaugurate a similar era of modernity: in fact, it was largely through borrowing from Islamic civilisation that Occidentals had been able to break the framework of traditional mediaeval thought and embark upon their Renaissance.

This problem connects with some of our earlier remarks on the tendencies of today's civilisation. For despite the ideas of many progressive Muslims, Western modernity, which was the logical cause of the present crisis, originated, in the final analysis, in a spirit which is the very negation of Islam and is even (to judge by the decline of the Churches) hard to reconcile with Christianity itself. Of course, it has achieved countless dazzling conquests in this world, but, deprived of transcendent principles, and thus of accord with Heaven, it has expedited the collapse of its own 'humanism' and has finished up with a generalised nihilism coupled with the threat of universal disaster. Muslim civilisation could never have taken the initiative in such a development without betraying itself, and it is this, finally, which explains why the modern world was born in Europe, not in the lands of Islam.

These remarks do not mean to imply that Islam sets its face against the progress of science and civilisation. From the time when the first Muslim armies surged forth from the deserts of Arabia, its whole history bears witness to the contrary. It does, however, impose limits upon everything which bears the label 'progress', bearing in mind the need to preserve the equilibrium of the created world and to leave man with a chance to accomplish the higher vocation to which God has called him. This is why it will always be in irreducible discord with the specifically modern outlook, to which the following Qur'anic passage applies perfectly: *They know only an aspect of the life of this world, and are in ignorance of the life which is to come.* (XXX:7)

SOURCE TEXTS

Science and Truth

Let man consider that from which he is created.
(Qur'an, LXXXVI:5)

Have they not reflected on the kingdom of the heavens and the earth, and what things God has made?
(VII:185)

Those who have been given knowledge see that what is revealed to you from your Lord is the truth, and leads to the path of the Almighty, the Owner of Praise. (XXXIV:6)

Do not follow that of which you have no knowledge. The hearing, the sight, the heart: of each of these it shall be questioned. (XVII:36)

God will exalt those who believe amongst you, and those who are given knowledge, to high ranks. God is All-Aware of what you do. (LVIII:11)

'Seek knowledge, though it be in China.'
Ḥadīth of the Prophet (upon whom be blessings and peace)

> The search for knowledge is a divinely instituted and general obligation. When some people discharge it, the others are relieved thereof, save that which concerns knowledge indispensible to every believer.
>
> Ibn Abī Zayd al-Qayrawānī, *Risāla* (a treatise on Islamic law according to the Mālikī rite.)

A misunderstood civilisation

Most Europeans have not fully appreciated the importance of the influence which they have received from Islamic civilisation, or the nature of their borrowings from it in the past; and there are some people who go so far as to disregard totally all that pertains to it. The reason is that the history which they have been taught makes a travesty of the facts, and appears in many respects to have been deliberately distorted. It is only with reserve that they deign to give any consideration to Islamic culture, being more used to denigrating it at every opportunity. One has to note that the historical teaching offered in European universities does not show the influences as they are. On the contrary, the truth which ought to be stated in their regard is systematically put aside, especially regarding the most important events.

For example, while it is generally known that Spain lived under the law of Islam for many centuries, it is never stated that the same was the case in other countries, such as Sicily and the south of France. There are some who would like to ascribe this silence on the part of the historians to some form of religious prejudice. But what are we to make of modern historians, most of whom have no religion, or are enemies of every religion, when they repeat the words of their ancestors, in manifest violation of the truth?

We are therefore forced to see in this one of the consequences of the arrogance and presumption of Westerners, through which they are prevented from recognising the truth and the scale of their debts to the Orient.

The most bizarre part of this phenomenon is the spectacle of Europeans regarding themselves as the direct heirs of Greek civilisation, although the facts themselves belie this pretence. The reality discernable in history itself establishes for all time that Greek science and philosophy were transmitted to the Europeans through Muslim intermediaries.

René Guénon in *Etudes Traditionelles*, December 1950

A serenity bordering on beatitude.

The stability of the institutions of Easterners, their resignation before events which have either happened or cannot be prevented, and the brotherhood which exists among all classes, offer a striking contrast to the endless revolutions, the agitated and feverish existence, and the social rivalries of the European peoples.

An extreme politeness and mildness, a fine tolerance of people and of things, calmness and dignity in all conditions and states, a high degree of moderation in their needs; these are the predominant characteristics of Oriental people. Their tranquil acceptance of life gives them a serenity of spirit very close to beatitude, while our aspirations and artificial needs have led us into a spirit of permanent disquiet which seems wholly remote from it.

Gustave Le Bon, *La Civilisation des Arabes*

Paradise concealed

A mosque generally comprises a court with a fountain, where the faithful can make their ablutions before accomplishing their prayers. The fountain is often protected by a small cupola shaped like a baldaquin. The court with a fountain in the middle, as well as the enclosed garden watered by four runnels rising in its centre, are made in the likeness of Paradise, for the Koran speaks of the gardens of Beatitude, where springs of water flow, one or two in each garden, and where celestial virgins dwell. It is in the nature of Paradise (*jannah*) to be hidden and secret; it corresponds to the interior world, the innermost soul. This is the world which the Islamic house must imitate, with its inner court surrounded with walls on all four sides or with an enclosed garden furnished with a well or fountain. The house is the *sacratum* (*haram*) of the family, where woman reigns and man is but a guest. Its square shape is in conformity with the Islamic law of marriage, which allows a man to marry up to four wives, on condition that he offers the same advantages to each. The Islamic house is completely closed towards the outer world—family life is withdrawn from the general social life—it is only open above, to the sky, which is reflected beneath in the fountain of the court.

Titus Burckhardt, *Sacred Art of East and West*

Libraries, treasuries of erudition

The library of the Samanid palace at Bukhara, we are told by Avicenna (d.1036), who worked there, consisted of a separate palace with several departments, each of which was filled with a great number of shelves ranged one above the other. Each department was set aside for a particular branch of scholarship: philology, poetry, law, and so forth. There was a subject catalogue. 'I saw some books in there', he exclaimed, 'which no-one has seen anywhere else.'

The finest library of all was that of al-Aziz (975–96) in Old Cairo. It contained 1,600,000 volumes, of which 6,500 concerned the mathematical sciences, and 18,000 dealt with philosophy. In this place one could admire, besides various astronomical instruments and orrery spheres, a huge *mappa mundi* of blue silk. 'It bore a painting of the continents, the oceans, the rivers, roads and mountains, and the holy and other cities, with their names written in characters of gold.' Al-Aziz bought hugely expensive books which were sent to him by his agents who were spread all over the world of Islam, and he possessed an immense collection of autographed manuscripts and works which were unique in all the world.

Al-Hakim (996–1021) founded, also in Old Cairo, a new library of 600,000 volumes, called the 'Palace of Knowledge'.

Aly Mazahéri, *La Vie Quotidienne des Musulmans au Moyen Age*

7

Spiritual paths and families

SPIRITUAL breadth and unity characterised the life of the first Muslim community created by the Prophet at Medina. Combining in his personality all the attributes of saintliness and human perfection, synthesising all the qualitative aspects of creation, he was what the mystics would one day call the Universal Man (*al-Insān al-Kāmil*). Ranged around him, his closest Companions were also saints worthy of their exalted situation, in the first rank of those to whom the revelation of Islam was addressed. Like the disciples of Christ, they were not always exempt from human failings, but they showed so many virtues and excellences in the service of God and His Messenger that, to the present day, Muslims continue to look on them as their exemplars and endeavour to walk in their footsteps.

Under the Prophet's four immediate successors, Abū Bakr, ʿUmar, ʿUthmān and ʿAlī, who are known today as the 'Orthodox Caliphs', or the 'Rightly-guided Caliphs' (*al-khulafā' al-rāshidūn*), the Muslim state remained the complete expression of the ideals of Islam and of their implementation in a human society. The community of believers possessed all the qualities and conditions which would allow the Prophet's religion to spread through the world with the same efficiency as it won souls for the Hereafter. The caliphs themselves were at once men of action, political leaders, and pre-eminent spiritual masters.

The first of these, Abū Bakr, who had been the most intimate friend of the Prophet, achieved a powerful combination of these two aspects of Islam, the exterior (*ẓāhir*) and the interior (*bāṭin*), which, in later times, were all too frequently divided. On the one hand he was a leader endowed with a remarkable political and even military acumen which allowed him to consolidate the authority of the young Muslim state and reinforce its structures, while at the same time laying down the foundations for the *fiqh*—Islamic jurisprudence—by formulating the principles of *Ijtihād*, 'personal endeavour in research'. On the other hand he was a 'mystic', if we understand by this term a man who has knowledge of 'mysteries'. This knowledge he transmitted to those who were worthy of it, and tradition tells us that he was the first to recommend the systematic practice of *dhikr*, the 'remembrance' and invocation of God. It is for this reason that the Sufi brotherhoods often trace their genealogies back to him, and through him to the Prophet himself.

The personality of ʿUmar ibn al-Khaṭṭāb has left even more profound traces on the Muslim consciousness, since his reign lasted for more than ten years, whereas Abū Bakr had been in power only for two years and a half. The second Caliph was gifted with an exceptionally forceful character which enabled him both to practise the highest public and personal virtues, and at the same time to implement in the community at large the great ideals of Islam to a degree which has never since been equalled.

ʿUmar led a life of extreme austerity, and, even when the conquests of his generals had made him the most powerful head of state in the Middle East, he continued to eat and dress as modestly as most of those whom he ruled. There is a famous episode concerning his arrival at Jerusalem, where he had come to receive the submission of the city: dressed in coarse clothes, he was escorted by a single servant and by one camel which he and his servant would take turns to ride. Tradition also speaks of many other examples of his total selflessness and his lively awareness of the equality of human beings in the sight of God. He accepted no privileges for himself, and forbade his governors, judges and employees from extending any preferential treatment to the rich and powerful. Thus he ordered the son of ᶜAmr ibn al-ᶜĀṣ, the conqueror of Egypt, to be lashed for having struck a Copt without reason.

The second caliph saw personally to the welfare of all, and directly looked after the conditions of life of the populace. It was his custom to roam the streets of Medina incognito and without an escort, asking people about their day-to-day problems and then taking steps to rectify them. He organised his administration in such a way as to submit everything to the principles of equity and solidarity, which he regarded as the major requirements of Islam, to the extent that modern Muslim reformers have been able to find no better model for their ideas of social justice. While insisting on these exterior and 'social' facets of religion, ᶜUmar bore witness also to an interior perfection which has provided the inspiration for generations of mystics.

The third and fourth caliphs exemplified the same fullness of human and spiritual qualities, both in their being and their actions. Although the chroniclers often report that ᶜUthmān showed an overly complaisant attitude toward his relatives, he was undeniably a man of exemplary nobility and generosity. His benevolence was proverbial, and he left a number of fine sayings which counsel kindness and moderation in human relationships.

As for ᶜAlī, regarded by the Shīᶜa as the most deserving of the four caliphs to succeed the Prophet, whose son-in-law and cousin he was, he was reproached by some for inadequacy in the political arena, but no-one can deny that he was—and incomparably so—both a man of action and of contemplation. A fearless and magnanimous warrior, he risked his life many times in the defence of Islam and its Prophet, who declared in a *ḥadīth* : 'I am the city of knowledge, and ᶜAlī is its gate'. It is hardly surprising, then, that the majority of the mystical streams of Islam should recognise him as their source.

The death of ᶜAlī signalled the close of that fortunate age when the leader of the believing community, firstly the Prophet, then each of the first four caliphs, possessed an intrinsic authority which was as much spiritual as temporal. It should be realised that the conflicts which broke out under the fourth caliph, and which set the faithful against one another, pertained neither to faith nor doctrine: they were political, being centred on the question of the caliphal succession. The Umayyads, who emerged victorious and assumed the caliphal title, were essentially political leaders, and, with the exception of ᶜUmar ibn ᶜAbdal-ᶜAzīz, whose reign was a last ephemeral manifestation of ideal Muslim government, were primarily temporal rulers, even though they continued to style themselves 'Commanders of the Faithful'.

It is from this period that the great ramifications of Islam date: Sunnism (85–90 percent of the world's Muslims), Shīᶜism (10–15 percent), and Khārijism, or Ibāḍism (numerically very weak). The fact should also be underlined that these have never been divided by real doctrinal differences, but rather by questions of the interpretation and application of the religious law, both on the individual and the collective level.

From that time forth, the norm of truth and of conformity to the revealed Message which one might designate as 'Muslim orthodoxy', established limits which individuals and groups might not transgress without being excluded from the *Umma*, the community of the Prophet. Even today, there are no theologians, even among the most modernistic, who debate the 'necessary beliefs'.*

Within these clearly and indisputably articulated boundaries there has developed, throughout Islam's long history, a large

* In an age in which one sees, even in some Christian theological circles, challenges made to facts such as the virginity of Mary, the miraculous birth of Christ or his ascension into heaven at the close of his earthly life, it is interesting to note that all Muslims accept, to the letter and without argument, these traditional data concerning *Sayyidinā ᶜĪsā* (Jesus), which are common ground for Islam and Christianity. There is no circumstance which better approximates to the claim sometimes heard from Muslims who say: 'We are the true Christians!'

number of currents and tendencies, which crystallised into assorted groups—a term which we will employ to translate the Arabic word *firqa* (plural *firaq*), to avoid the word 'sect' which is always liable to misinterpretation. Since each one obviously claims the greater degree of fidelity to the original Message, or to give it the most correct, full or profound interpretation, polemics have been inevitable. They have been frequently and ardently expressed, sometimes reaching the point of mutual anathema. Even today these discords are far from being resolved, and, between many groups, suspicion has not vanished entirely.

By and large, though, these various collectivities have constantly referred back to the privileged and exemplary era of the Prophet and the 'rightly-guided' caliphs, although with differing emphases: some attaching themselves primarily to the social and exterior aspects of the primitive *Dār al-Islām*, while others have quested for a more spiritual, interior perfection. The former tendency has manifested itself in numerous reformist theological and philosophical schools, while the second has been, and continues to be, that of the mystics and the Sufis. At times there has been opposition and incomprehension between the two, although, after the time of Ghazālī (d.1111), it became hard to deny that both were integral and irreplaceable components of the most authentic version of Islam.

Meanwhile, contact with other civilisations and the impinging intellectual heritage of classical antiquity opened new avenues for Muslim thought, which, from these foreign sources, adopted those elements which were compatible with its own perspective, integrating them into one of the two major tendencies which we have just described. In this way there developed in the Abbasid period, under the influence of Hellenistic philosophy, and more particularly that of Plato and Aristotle which had been made accessible through the labours of the Arab translators, the intellectual current known as the *falsafa*. Some of the most illustrious names of Arab-Muslim civilisation, such as al-Kindī, al-Fārābī,

Ibn Sīnā (Avicenna), and Ibn Rushd (Averroes), were ranked among the *falāsifa* ('philosophers'), who eventually found themselves in opposition to the doctors of *kalām* (apologetic theology), who considered their thought too 'profane' and too heavily dependent on non-Islamic sources.

The *kalām* incorporated two main tendencies. The first of these was that of the Muᶜtazilites, who, stressing the concept of human free will, have often been called the 'rationalists' of Islam. They saw themselves as defenders of Muslim doctrine against the excessive impact of ancient philosophy, while appealing, like the philosophers themselves, to the resources of reason. Asserting that the Qur'an is a direct creation by God, they were fought from the tenth century onwards by a school founded by the theologian Abu'l-Ḥasan al-Ashᶜarī, who proclaimed the uncreated nature of the revealed Book and the inaccessibility of the divine mystery. The Ashᶜarites emerged victorious from the fray, and ever since, Muslim theology has taught that the Qur'an, God's Word, is uncreated. On other points of doctrine, however, such as the use of reason to defend the faith, Ashᶜarism still provoked various reservations and disagreements, particularly on the part of the Ḥanafī and Ḥanbalī theologians; nevertheless, these were minor divergences to which most believers were largely indifferent.

In a general way, Sunni theology remained faithful to the Qur'anic verse which announces: *We have made of you a middle nation* (II:143), which some translators render as 'far from extremes', and which clearly encapsulates a trait of the most genuine form of Islam. However, the movements which have unsettled the Muslim world down the centuries were doubtless not all inspired by this ideal of the 'golden mean', and some have generated various forms of extremism. Mention should be made in particular of the 'Qarmatian revolution' which, in the tenth century, shook Abbasid power to its foundations. Linked to the Ismāᶜīlī brand of Shīᶜism, but having adopted various doctrinal elements alien to Islam, the Qarmatians attacked the existing social order and practiced a sort of communism in the state which they founded in al-Ḥaṣā, a region of northwestern Arabia. Other groups springing from the same branch of Shīʿism manifested themselves in due course, and some, like the Druzes and Alawites, still exist today in the Near East.

Nostalgia for the initial age of Islam inspired other movements which, at various moments in history, expressed a determination to return to the original purity of the faith by eliminating 'innovations' (*bidʿa*), which were regarded as deviations from the good tradition (*sunna*) of the Prophet. Very often these reformers were of nomadic origin, hailing from the deserts or the mountains, which is why the restoration of Sunnism in the East was to a great extent the work of dynasties of Turkish or Kurdish stock.

In North Africa it was similarly the non-Arab chiefs who became champions of Sunni Islam. Pouring over the Sahara from the confines of Senegal, the Almoravids (*al-murābiṭūn*, or 'people of the fortified retreats') made themselves masters of all North Africa and Muslim Spain, where they imposed a strict application of the Mālikī school of law. It was their leader, Yūsuf ibn Tāshfīn, who founded the city of Marrakesh in 1070. In the next century, however, a Berber tribe appeared from the High Atlas under a new reformer, Ibn Tūmart, who preached a return to the sources of Islam and an uncompromising interpretation of *tawḥīd*, the doctrine of Divine Unity. He also announced that he was the *mahdī*, who, according to a variety of traditions, must one day establish a reign of justice on the earth. His disciples styled themselves *al-muwaḥḥidūn*, the 'unitarians', from which term the name of their Almohad dynasty was derived, and which dominated the extreme west of the Muslim world until the second half of the thirteenth century.

This 'spirit of reform', often associated with the anticipation of the *mahdī*, has never wholly vanished from the Muslim consciousness. It has often taken on a 'fundamentalist' character based on a literal interpretation of the Qur'an and *Sunna*, seeking to restore an Islam purified of all innovations which fail to conform strictly to the letter of the revelation.

In the modern period this tendency has found a particularly zealous expression in Wahhābism, a religious movement dating from the eighteenth century which remains remarkably active and influential even today. It has been, and continues to be, the inspiration for the Saudi dynasty which today holds sway over most of the Arabian peninsula.

Muḥammad ibn ʿAbd al-Wahhāb, from whom the movement takes its name, was born in the Najd region of Central Arabia at the beginning of the eighteenth century. After studying the Ḥanbalī school of law, he travelled for some time in Iraq and Iran. He was particularly influenced by the 'neo-Hanbalism' of the great theologian Ibn Taymiyya, who, four centuries earlier, had spoken out against a number of practices which he considered incompatible with pristine Islam, such as the veneration of saints and the visitation of their graves; he had also fought energetically against both the philosophers on one hand, and the Sufis and the mystics on the other.

Ibn ʿAbd al-Wahhāb took this tendency even further, preaching a rigorist Islam based on the literal application of the *Sharīʿa*. He gained the support of a growing number of disciples, who, professing an uncompromising *tawḥīd*, applied to themselves the term *al-muwaḥḥidūn*. The new community found a patron in the emir Muḥammad ibn Saʿūd, hereditary chieftain of a principality in Najd, who transformed his domains into the first state which could legitimately be termed Wahhābī.

During the first years of the nineteenth century, the son and successor of Muḥammad ibn Saʿūd, ʿAbd al-ʿAzīz, driven by the urge to purify and revive the Islamic world by subjecting it to the Wahhābī principles and rules of life, unleashed a military campaign which brought his warriors through one of the most remarkable military adventures which Arabia had seen since the time of the Prophet and the first caliphs. Achieving spectacular successes, the Wahhābī troops quickly subjugated almost all of Arabia, and then, thrusting northwards, soon found themselves before the walls of Baghdad and Damascus. The Ottoman caliph realised the threat, and called upon the recently modernised army of his Egyptian viceroy, which, after a long and difficult campaign, gained the upper hand over the Wahhābī military power. The Wahhābī commander, ʿAbdallāh ibn Saʿūd, was taken captive and was later executed at Istanbul. To all appearances, the sect had been crushed for good.

In the central and eastern regions of Arabia, however, the Wahhābī faith remained alive, and it was this which, at the outset of the twentieth century, made possible the rebirth of the Saʿūdī state and animated the warriors of a new ʿAbd al-ʿAzīz, whom the West knows as Ibn Saʿūd. In 1924 he captured the two most holy places of Islam, and proclaimed, in 1932, the Kingdom of Saudi Arabia, in which Wahhābī austerity was enforced. All the tombs of the saints, which were very numerous in the region, were destroyed, and all practices which were thought to be superstitious were banned. Nevertheless, law and order did prevail, and pilgrims travelling to Mecca and Medina could count on being completely secure.

Wahhābism has maintained its dominant position in Saudi Arabia under the successors of ʿAbd al-ʿAzīz. The kingdom's constantly growing contact with the outside world has tended, nevertheless, to make it more flexible and less rigorous.

Following Ibn Taymiyya, the Wahhābīs have always been opposed to the various forms of mysticism usually subsumed under the rubric of Sufism, and this interdiction is palpable in the Saudi state. In this regard they find themselves in accord with certain other reformist currents which have appeared in the Muslim world since the last century, but which had already become more tainted with modernism. The *Salafī* movement (the '*salaf*' being the early Muslims), as incarnated in such personalities as Jamāl al-Dīn al-Afghānī and Muḥammad ʿAbduh, and which wields its deepest influence in Egypt and Syria, also perceives itself as a return to the pristine purity of Islam, but at the same time endeavours to reconcile the faith to modern Western values. This has naturally induced it to oppose the Sufi brotherhoods, which it accuses of degenerate and superstitious practices such as maraboutism. Some of these reformers have gone so far as to declare that mysticism itself is alien to Islam, and regard it as the result of a corruption inspired by external influences.*

In reality, authentic Sufism, which has little enough to do with maraboutism or the spectacle of certain other eccentricities presented by some brotherhoods, consists mainly in a deepening and interiorisation of Islam. It does not, therefore, need to manifest itself externally in order to exist authentically, which is why it can be difficult even to discern its presence. What is certain, however, is that it has always exercised an attraction for those contemplative souls who yearn for spiritual perfection.

The term 'Sufism' (*taṣawwuf*) derives from the cloak of wool (*ṣūf*) often worn by the mystics of the first centuries. They themselves were usually known by the term 'the poor' (*fuqarā'*, the plural of *faqīr*, in Persian *darvīsh*, which have given us the English words 'fakir' and 'dervish'), in a reference to the verse of the Qur'an which declares: *You are the poor before God, and God is the Rich* (XXXV:15). The 'poverty' in question refers to the spiritual attitude of detachment which flows from preferring the next world to the goods of this, and in the extinction of man before the Divine Reality.

Sufism, according to its own spokesmen, existed well before it was designated by any specific label, since it was, in a way, implicit in the time of the Prophet, whose Companions realised the spiritual ideals of Islam far more completely than the Muslims of

* This opinion used to be supported by numerous Western orientalists, who saw in Muslim mysticism all manner of Christian, Mazdean, Hindu and other influences. It has lost much of its credit following the work of scholars such as Massignon on the Islamic origins of Sufism.

later generations. Moreover the Qur'an and the Ḥadīths abound in mystical teachings to which the Sufis make reference in order to show that they follow a path flowing directly from the Revelation.

The figure who is usually seen as standing at the head of the great spiritual family tree of Sufism is al-Ḥasan al-Baṣrī (from Basra in southern Iraq), born in Medina during the reign of the caliph ʿUmar, who once took him into his arms. Tradition relates that he heard the teachings of ʿAlī, the Prophet's son-in-law, and that his whole life was given over to their practice. His reputation for saintliness spread throughout the Islamic state, and he was the only man who dared remonstrate with the Umayyad caliphs, who were often notorious for their impiety. ʿUmar ibn ʿAbdal-ʿAzīz, who by his great virtue formed an exception among members of the dynasty, drew his inspiration from the counsels of al-Ḥasan, who once wrote the following letter to him from Basra: 'Beware of this world with all wariness; for it is like to a snake, smooth to the touch, but its venom is deadly. Turn away from whatsoever delights thee in it, for the little companioning thou wilt have of it.'* Al-Ḥasan also declared: 'He that knoweth God loveth Him, and he that knoweth the world abstaineth from it.'* These few words sum up an essential aspect of the Sufi way.

Also living at Basra during the second Hegira century was Rābiʿa al-ʿAdawiyya, a deeply influential woman saint to whom numerous miracles are ascribed. A former slave and flute-player, she lived an ascetic existence devoted entirely to the selfless and exclusive love of God. She wrote mystical poems ('You have I made the Companion of my heart'), which the 'thirsty for God' have always delighted to recite.

Other mystics soon appeared even in the most remote provinces of Islam. One of the most remarkable of these was Ibrāhīm ibn Adham (eighth century), the scion of a princely family of

* Cited by A.J. Arberry, *Sufism*.

† Martin Lings, *What is Sufism?*

Balkh in Afghanistan. Many edifying stories are related of him, and he is also credited with miracles. But one key word in his spirituality was *faqr*, 'poverty', for his was a way of total renunciation. 'Poverty', he would say, 'is a treasure kept by God in Heaven, which He grants only to those He loves.' Disciples were drawn to him, and a 'spiritual lineage' often termed the 'mystical school of Khurasan' came into being, which honoured the virtues of poverty, trust and surrender (*tawakkul*) to the Divine Will, together with the methodical practice of *dhikr*, the remembrance, or repetition, of the Divine Name.

Other Sufis emphasised the idea of the knowledge of God, or, if one prefers, of 'gnosis' (*maʿrifa*). This was the case with Dhu'l-Nūn al-Miṣrī, ('the Egyptian', who died in 861), who left behind a number of treatises and poems into which pantheist tendencies have wrongly been read by some Orientalists: 'O God, I never hearken to the voices of the beasts or the rustle of the trees, the splashing of waters or the song of birds, the whistling of the wind or the rumble of thunder, but that I sense in them a testimony to Thy unity!'*

It was at Baghdad, however, that the best-known Sufis lived, and where their fame was often fed by controversies which flared up around them. Generally ascribing themselves to the spiritual inheritance of al-Ḥasan al-Baṣrī, they exercised a vast influence throughout the Abbasid empire, and it is impossible to deny their central place in the history of Islam and the elaboration of its religious thought.

Among the most eminent Sufis was al-Junayd, who effectively functioned as the school's leader. He left behind a great number of teachings, including this definition: 'Sufism is God's causing you to die to yourself and to live in Him'. He insisted on the necessity of remaining strictly faithful to the path of the Prophet: 'All mystical ways are closed, except to him who follows in the

* Cited by Arberry, *Sufism*.

footsteps of the Messenger.'* At the same time, however, he advised his disciples 'not to speak to excess', and to avoid making any statement which might be misunderstood and cause scandal outside Sufi circles.

Al-Junayd's advice was not always followed, and a situation of discord arose with the religious authorities, who condemned several Sufis for having used language which they considered impious and heretical. The most notorious instance of this was the case of Manṣūr al-Ḥallāj. It should be noted, none the less, that the authorities had their reasons for being on their guard, since they were aware that a serious threat could be presented by heterodox movements and sects, such as Qarmatism, which had appeared in the first centuries of Islam; and the untimely words of some Sufis appeared to them to be the harbingers of a comparable danger.

Many theological schools, however, came to acknowledge Sufism, a fact due in large part to the influence of the famous scholar and philosopher al-Ghazālī (1058–1111), often styled *Ḥujjat al-Islām*, the 'Proof of Islam'. A renowned theologian and jurist, his authoritative teaching at Baghdad was interrupted by a crisis of doubt, during which, as he relates in his autobiography, he started to question all his learning and all the doctrines of religion. He rediscovered certainty after directly experiencing the Truth according to the way of the mystics, and thenceforth taught that Sufism provided the most effective weapon against doubt and unbelief.†

Even though a few particularly strict and rigorous theologians remained critical of his work, Ghazālī's prestige in general allowed the Sufis to reconcile themselves with official orthodoxy.

* Cited by Lings, *What is Sufism?*

† His return to faith was assisted also by reading the *Qūt al-Qulūb* (*Sustenance of Hearts*) of Abū Ṭālib al-Makkī, and the works of al-Muḥāsibī. Quotations from Junayd, Shiblī, Abū Yazīd al-Bisṭāmī and other Sufis fill the pages of his own writings.

Although it still gave rise to periodic objections, *taṣawwuf* was recognised, could develop more freely, and gave birth to a variety of orders and brotherhoods which came to provide an irreplaceable vitality of spiritual life in the majority of Muslim countries.

In the next generation in Baghdad there lived a master who was called upon to radiate an immense influence, and who even today is claimed by innumerable believers: ʿAbd al-Qādir al-Jīlānī (1077–1166), known as the 'Sultan of the Saints' on account of his spiritual calibre. A powerful orator, he drew great crowds to whom he communicated his fervour, calling them to repent, to practice *dhikr*, and to practice the virtues. Jews and Christians converted to Islam after hearing him, and the miracles attributed to him, particularly the healing of the sick, were innumerable. His poems celebrating mystical intoxication and divine love have thrilled multitudes of souls, and are recited even today:

> Praised be my drunkenness, permitted the nectar
> which has no origin in the vine or its fruit.
> At the divine cup which I raise to my lips,
> one sip is quaffed, and my soul sways
> In an ecstasy whose fire is never quenched.
> Love! Once it reaches the lover's heart
> Dark night flares for its sake . . .*

ʿAbd al-Qādir, who was also a fine theologian, and who adhered faithfully to the laws and practices of Islam, never collided with the religious authorities, but used his unchallenged spiritual authority to 'clear' Sufism definitively, thus consummating the work begun by Ghazālī. Regarded as the patron saint of Baghdad, where his tomb draws numerous visitors, he remains one of the most popular saints of Islam, and the *ṭarīqa* which bears his name is probably the most widespread Sufi order in the Muslim world.

* Mehmed Ali Aïni, *Abd-al-Kadir Guilani.*

During this era of spiritual renewal in a civilisation which stood at the zenith of its splendour, many other saints lived in the most diverse provinces of Islam, notably in the far west. Today there is the ever-living memory of Abū Madyan Shuᶜayb, a native of Spain, who travelled to Baghdad in order to meet ᶜAbd al-Qādir al-Jīlānī, after which he retraced his steps to North Africa. Buried near the city of Tlemçen, where his tomb is a venerated monument, he is often regarded as the patron saint of Algeria.*

Also of Andalusian origin was Muḥyi'd-Dīn ibn ᶜArabī (1165–1240), the author of a number of Sufi works which mostly expound the doctrine of the 'Unity of Being' (*waḥdat al-wujūd*), a thesis which remains challenged by the most classical form of Muslim theology. It has nevertheless wielded considerable influence, as is attested by his soubriquet of *ash-shaykh al-akbar*, the 'Greatest Shaykh', which is often given him, and which is still used to refer to the mosque at Damascus which adjoins his tomb.†

Another influential saint was Abu'l-Hasan al-Shādhilī (1196–1258), who was forced to leave his native Tunis where the authorities had become jealous of his prestige, and passed a large part of his life at Alexandria. His master was ᶜAbd al-Salām ibn Mashīsh, who lies buried near Chaouen in the Moroccan Rif mountains, and who himself had been a disciple of Abū Madyan. His teaching was as widespread as it was durable, and the prayers which he composed remain in use in a vast spiritual family which derives from him in North Africa and the Near East. He was the effective founder of a *ṭarīqa* which, in the number of its adherents, may almost rival that of al-Jīlānī.

* Abū Madyan ('Boumédiènne') was the name adopted during the Algerian War of Independence by the future president of that country.

† Emir ᶜAbd al-Qādir, the heroic defender of Algeria against the French invasion of the nineteenth century, who passed the latter years of his life at Damascus, and who was also an eminent Sufi, was buried beside the tomb of Ibn ᶜArabī. After the independence of Algeria was regained, his remains were translated to his native land.

Among his disciples mention should be made of Ibn ʿAṭā'illāh (d.1309), the author of a famous collection of aphorisms (*al-Ḥikam*: 'the Wisdoms') which continues to be highly popular today both in Arabic and in translations which have been made of it into other Islamic languages such as Turkish and Malay. He was an ardent defender of mysticism, as is shown by his polemics against Ibn Taymiyya.

Apart from the two great orders of the Qādirīya and the Shādhilīya, many other brotherhoods, or *ṭuruq* (the plural of *ṭarīqa*, a 'spiritual path'), were founded during the same period. Particularly influential in India and Pakistan is that which traces back its lineage to Muʿīn al-Dīn Chishtī (d.1236), who, through his spiritual influence, made a very substantial contribution to the spread of Islam. Numerous visitors, many of them non-Muslims, continue to visit and meditate at his tomb in Ajmer in Rajasthan.

The Mawlawī *ṭarīqa* (*mevlevī* in Turkish) is somewhat better known in the West, thanks to its famous 'whirling dervishes'. Descended from Jalāl al-Dīn Rūmī (1207–73), a saint whose immense authority has continued throughout the centuries, its influence in the Ottoman Empire extended beyond the bounds of religion and entered the arena of politics. Rūmī's principle vocation, however, was to call men to the love of God (*maḥabba*), and to renew their ardour. His works, most particularly the *Mathnawī* (composed of forty-five thousand verses), which have set him among the greatest mystical poets of all time, continue to inspire Muslim piety and to guide souls which yearn to deepen and interiorise their faith.

> Love is an infinite ocean in which the heavens are no more than a flock of foam.
>
> Know that it is the waves of Love which turn the wheels of heaven; without Love, the world would be without life.
>
> Each atom is infatuated with this Perfection, and

hastens towards it. Their haste says implicitly, 'Glory to God!'

(God says:) 'If it were not by pure love, then how would I have given existence to the heavens?

I raised up this sublime celestial sphere so that you might know how sublime is Love.'*

To name all of the *turuq* and their subdivisions would require several pages, revealing how deeply the mysticism which they represent is rooted in all the Muslim peoples. But let us cite a specifically Asian brotherhood, that of the Naqshbandīya, founded in the fourteenth century by Bahā' ad-Dīn Naqshband of Bukhara, which is widespread in Turkestan, among the Soviet Tatars, in Turkey, in China, India and Java. It is only one example among many which show that Islam owes its progress more to brotherhoods who win over hearts than to missionary propaganda or other forms of influence.

A much more recent era saw the founding of a brotherhood which is somewhat different in character, particularly in view of the influence which it wielded in the struggle against Western colonial oppression. A native of Algeria, its founder, Muḥammad ibn ʿAlī as-Sanūsī (1791–1859), was a member of the Qādirī *ṭarīqa*, and later founded, following a sojourn in Mecca, the order which bears his name, which became very numerous in many parts of North Africa and the Sahara. Under his son and successor Sayyid Muḥammad, popularly known as the 'Great Sanūsī', the whole, thus constituted, became an important theocratic desert empire which firmly applied the traditional religious prescriptions and proved a powerful impulse towards popular education. It is interesting to note that while it was rooted in *taṣawwuf*, the Sanūsī Order was not without certain external similarities to Wahhābism, particularly with regard to its military vocation, its moral austerity, and its spirit of sacrifice.

*Quoted by Eva de Vitray-Meyerovitch, *Rumi and Sufism*, Post-Apollo.

In other circumstances, various brotherhoods—or at least the vestiges of them—may have created the impression that Sufism in our day is in a state of irretrievable decline. Such has been the opinion of the Muslim reformist milieux, as also of certain orientalists. The reality is perhaps rather different and, without denying that decadence has discredited many *ṭuruq*, particularly those which have made too many concessions to popular or political tendencies, there is no shortage of indications to suggest that *taṣawwuf* is still alive and well.

Being, as we have stated, an interior aspect of Islam, and hence an esoterism, Sufism may in theory exist without manifesting itself on the surface in any way. In fact, however, its presence is noticeable in most Muslim countries, where many eminent personalities declare their affiliation to one *ṭarīqa* or another, the rules and spiritual practices of which they follow in order to deepen their faith. And although it represents a form of spirituality which is wholly foreign, even contrary, to the modern outlook, it is not uncommon to find graduates of Western training who have returned to it in order to evict the intellectual confusion of the modern world from their minds. If one also takes into account all the books which have appeared on the subject, one may affirm that Sufism is not yet devoid of its resources of *baraka*—spiritual influence—which it has channelled onwards since its early days, and that its influence remains a significant feature of Islam today.

Likewise, it seems certain that the Sufi masters have not wholly disappeared from the Muslim community of our time, and that they continue to gather around themselves souls which long to progress on the mystical path to God. One of the most eminent of these twentieth century Sufis was the Algerian shaykh Aḥmad al-ᶜAlawī of Mostaghanem, whose influence and sanctity drew numerous disciples not only from North Africa, but from other African countries and from the Middle East as well. He was comparable in many ways to the great Sufis of the classical period, some of whose names we have mentioned, and, until his death in 1934, was a living proof of the perennial vigour of this spiritual tradition.

Even nowadays, the great mystic lineages of Islam are by no means all defunct, and masters, sometimes even saints, carry on the work. None the less, in an increasingly secularised world, there are doubtless more reasons than ever before for them to shun publicity.

As it has continued to do since the time of al-Ḥasan al-Baṣrī, Sufi teaching requires from its disciples a general attitude of spiritual poverty (*faqr*): a detachment from the world, which is the indispensable condition for true engagement on the Path (*ṭarīqa*). This requires spiritual exercises to be observed in addition to the strict performance of all the canonical obligations of the faith, and may be summarised in one word which refers to an essential aspect of Islam, and which has already been cited many times in the preceding pages: *dhikr*, the remembrance, mention, recollection or invocation of God.

In a way (as we have already noted) every one of Islam's practices is a *dhikr*, since its rites by definition involve the ceaseless affirmation and remembrance of the divine Unity, as do the traditional Muslim forms of life, which are always centred on the essential theme of the return to the One. But Sufism has made *dhikr* into a specific and methodical practice based on numerous Qur'anic references, in particular the following: *Truly, the (ritual) prayer prevents that which is corrupt and reprehensible, and truly, the invocation* (dhikr) *of God is greater still* (XXIV:45). As a result, the Sufi way leads its followers to centre their lives on the invocation of God and the repetition of His name. This practice of *dhikr* may be solitary and silent, or done collectively during gatherings (*majālis*, plural of *majlis*) during the course of which the rhythmic repetition of the Divine Name, or other sacred formulas such as the *Shahāda*, are accompanied, in some *ṭuruq*, by drumbeats. On occasion the *dhikr* is punctuated by bodily movements, and forms a sacred dance, of which Rūmī's 'whirling dervishes' provide the best-known example. Sometimes it also leads to states of ecstasy, which are, however, disapproved of by the more stringent exponents of Muslim orthodoxy.

Sufi method often also includes exercises of meditation (*fikr*) aimed at penetrating the most profound truth (*ḥaqiqa*) of Islam. It demands an irreproachable conduct, the scrupulous practice of the virtues, and a constant struggle against the dispersing tendencies of the soul which hold the *faqīr* back from progressing towards the unique Centre.

Traditional doctrine teaches that the Muslim nature includes three fundamental elements: *islām*, surrender or submission to the Divine Will; *īmān*, faith in God and His Messenger, and *iḥsān*, 'virtue', 'sincerity', or 'excellence'. The Sufi masters always lay particular emphasis on *iḥsān*, believing it to be identical to *taṣawwuf*.

A *ḥadīth* of the Prophet gives this famous definition: '*Iḥsān* is to worship God as though you saw Him; and if you do not see Him, yet He sees you.' This formula summarises the entire path of the Sufis, which is 'worship' in the most profound sense of the word, and the realisation of the omnipresence of God.

Although Sufism is an inward (*bāṭin*) path destined primarily for contemplatives, its influence is nevertheless felt strongly on the outward (*ẓāhir*) level of action in this world, and to ignore it is to be unable to grasp the real significance of many political and social events in Muslim history. Even in the twentieth century it has often inspired movements for the defence of traditional Islam against the inroads of Western modernism. In Turkey, for instance, it is said that the *ṭuruq* have been the soul of the resistance to Ataturk's project of secularisation. If we except brotherhoods which are more or less decadent, particularly those which in certain regions compromised themselves with the colonial powers, it seems undeniable that Sufism remains one of the sources of inspiration of what the West labels, with some agitation, the advent of 'Muslim fundamentalism'.

The 'fundamentalist' tendency, which may also develop separately from any influence from the *ṭuruq*, has found its most important expression in the movement of the Muslim Brothers (*al-Ikhwān al-Muslimīn*), founded in 1928 at Cairo by Ḥasan al-Bannā. Despite being the victim of repressive measures, the movement exercises considerable influence in Egypt, and has gained many sympathisers not just in the Arab world, but also in Pakistan and Indonesia. It remains very representative of a popular attachment to traditional Islam and of resistance to 'progressist' and 'leftist' influences from Western or 'socialist' countries, and to all other modern and secularising forces.

Such notions of 'left' and 'right', however, cannot be applied in the world of Islam without a number of caveats. Despite the 'socialist' tag attached to some governments and the policies which they claim to implement, Muslim society, which is far less secularised than that of the West, remains resistant to specifically modernist ideologies, as well as to the myriad forms of antitraditional and subversive activism. Its faithfulness to the practice of religion contrasts starkly with the crises which are currently shaking Christianity (heterodox sects remaining limited in extent*), and the heralds of progress (whether Marxist or otherwise) and of a new golden age created by the works of man rather than by divine intervention, are little heeded by the popular masses, who prefer to hear the shaykhs and the imams who preach a return to the Islam of the first Caliphs. Of course, Muslims do

* The most notorious of the sects which have appeared recently is the Aḥmadiyya, which was founded at the close of the last century by an Indian Muslim, Mirzā Aḥmad of Qadiān in the Punjab. He professed many ideas which are unacceptable to orthodoxy regarding the mission of the Prophet, claiming that the *mahdī* would be a simultaneous reapparition of Jesus and Muhammad, and a new avatar of Krishna. The Aḥmadī community, whose members practice the rites of Islam, pursue a fairly substantial missionary operation in the West, where they have opened several mosques. Bahā'ism is a new religion founded by Persians of Muslim origin, but which has nothing in common with Islam.

welcome forms of progress which improve the conditions of their material lives, and restore their dignity before other nations, but they do not endow this notion with the ideological connotations which it carries in the West.*

In each of his ritual prayers, the Muslim addresses himself to God with the words, '*King of Judgement-day*'. Throughout the community of believers, this constantly repeated formula supports an awareness of the inexorable end which awaits all men, and upon which Islam has laid great stress ever since the earliest days of its revelation. It reminds them ceaselessly of the relativeness of this world, urging them not to place all their hopes therein, and thereby creates a vision of the future which is profoundly different from that of the secular progressism adhered to by the modern West under the influence of the evolutionist philosophies of the nineteenth century, and which remains the ideological basis of its civilisation. In this regard, as in so many others, the Muslim cannot be as truly and fully 'modern' as his Western counterpart; if he becomes so, then he ceases to be Muslim.

Awareness of the final Hour is readily associated with eschatological traditions which, although not Qur'anic, must be cited, if only briefly, beginning with the most ominous: a malevolent creature, the *Dajjāl*, a great impostor and negator who corresponds to the Antichrist of the Apocalypse, must come and sow falsehood, disorder and discord in the world. It is said that he will accomplish

* The French original of this book was in press when the late Ayatollah Khomeini's revolution erupted in Iran. It was not, as a result, possible to make reference to it, although the author has dealt with it extensively in two more recent works: *L'Islam entre tradition et révolution* (Paris: Tougui, 1987), and *Le réveil de l'Islam* (Paris: Cerf, 1988). Analysing the contradictory character of the expression 'Islamic revolution', which has been condemned by many traditional ulema, he reveals the powerful influence of modern Western ideologies upon the writings of the ideologues of so-called 'revolutionary Islam'. Having himself spent time in Iran in 1984, he believes that the regime which emerged from the 1979 revolution represented not a regeneration, but a drastic perversion of the Islamic faith. (Trans.)

all manner of prodigies, and that the great numbers of men whom he shall win over will revert to idolatry, and commit every form of vice and depravity.

There are many Muslims who, while accepting this belief, hold that the 'Dajjāl' will not be a personified entity, but is instead a reference to modern civilisation as such, which, through the almost miracle-like creatures of its technology, its false promises and its divisive spirit, turns men aside from the path of truth and salvation. According to another opinion, it refers to an individual who will appear as a personification of all the deception and revolt of the world in its final stages, and will preside over their paroxysmic climax.

However this may be, the earth shall be given up to the forces of evil and to the calamities unchained by the blasphemous hordes of Gog and Magog (*Yājūj* and *Mājūj*, mentioned twice in the Qur'an). Yet a leader shall appear, the *mahdī*, who shall defeat the enemies of God, and prepare for the return of Jesus, the son of Mary, after which they shall both cause the religion of the Prophet Muhammad to prevail, to which they themselves will adhere, re-establishing thereby the rule of truth and justice.

The circumstances of these final events which have been proclaimed by the eschatological traditions are described in more or less divergent versions, and it is not an obligation to believe in any of them. What matters is that Muslims agree on the final restoration of the divine order and the supreme triumph of Islam—taken in its highest sense—just as there is complete certainty concerning the Judgement (*al-Qiyāma*), the end of time, the conclusion of all things and the manifestation of the absolute sovereignty of the Almighty.

'And God knows best'. *Wa'Llāhu aʿlam*

SOURCE TEXTS

The Last Trump

They have not esteemed God as is His right.

The whole earth shall be in His hand on the Day of Resurrection, and the heavens shall be rolled in His right hand.

Glorified is He, and Exalted, above what they associate unto Him!

And the Trumpet shall be blown, and all who are in the heavens and the earth shall swoon, save those whom God wills.

Then shall it be blown again, and lo! they stand beholding.

The earth shines forth with the light of her Lord; the Book is set up; the Prophets and the witnesses are brought; and all are judged with equity, and none shall be wronged.

Each soul is paid in full for what it did, and He is best aware of what they used to do.

(Qur'an, XXXIX:67–70)

The love of God

Some there be among mankind who take unto themselves rivals to God, loving them as He alone should be loved. But those who believe are stauncher in their love for God.

Had those that work evil only known, when they beheld the chastisement, that power belongs wholly to

God, and that God is severe in punishment!
(Qur'an, II:165)

Say: Follow me, if you love God; He shall love you, and forgive you your wrong actions. He is the Forgiving, the Merciful. (Qur'an, III:31)

The sweetness of faith

The Prophet (may blessings and peace be upon him) has said: 'Whosoever possesses these three qualities has tasted the sweetness of faith:
– to love God and His Prophet more than all else.
– to love one's neighbour for the love of God.
– to loath to return to unbelief after God had saved one from it as much as one would loath to be thrown into the fire of hell.'

Teachings of the Rightly-guided Caliphs

Abū Bakr:

'Long for death and prepare for it as best you can, and life shall become for you like a generous gift.'

'The behaviour of the best of the servants of God shows itself in four ways: he rejoices when a sinner repents, he implores God to pardon those who do not even dream of repentance, he prays God to come to the aid of the unfortunate, and he helps all who do good.'

ᶜUmar ibn al-Khaṭṭāb:

'Beware of a surfeit of chattels which make life easy for you, just as much as you beware of disobeying God. In my sight, wealth is to be feared more than sin, since it can lead a man to destruction by imperceptible degrees by using all the seductions of which it is capable.'

ᶜUthmān ibn ᶜAffān:

'Everything has its own misfortune, every piece of good luck brings its own disgrace. The misfortune brought by this religion, the grief which accompanies the gift which it represents for us, is the critics and the slanderers. They show you exactly what you want to see, and conceal from you the faults which you would find it unpleasant to consider.'

ᶜAlī ibn Abī Ṭālib:

'Your souls are precious, and can be equal only to the price of Paradise; therefore sell them only at that price.

Whosoever struggles against the truth is soon cut down by it.'

Cited by René Khawam, *Propos des arabes sur la vie en sociètè*, Albin Michel.

The experience of the mystic Way

I apprehended clearly that the mystics were men who had real experiences, not men of words, and that I had already progressed as far as was possible by way of intellectual apprehension. What remained for me was not to be attained by oral instruction and study but only by immediate experience and by walking in the mystic way.

Now from the sciences I had laboured at and the paths I had traversed in my investigation of the revelational and rational sciences, there had come to me a sure faith in God, in prophethood, and in the Last Day. These three credal principles were firmly rooted in my being, not through any carefully argued proofs, but by reason of various causes, coincidences and experiences which are not capable of being stated in detail.

It had already become clear to me that I had no hope of the bliss of the world to come save through a God-fearing life and the withdrawal of myself from vain desire. It was clear to me too that the key to all this was to sever the attachment of the heart to worldly things by leaving the mansion of deception and returning to that of eternity, and to advance towards God with all earnestness. It was also clear that this was only to be achieved by turning away from wealth and position and fleeing from all time-consuming entanglements.

Next I considered the circumstances of my life, and realized that I was caught in a veritable thicket of attachments. I also considered my activities, of which the best was my teaching and lecturing, and realized that in them I was dealing with sciences that were unimportant and contributed nothing to the attainment of eternal life. (. . .)

I continued at this stage for the space of ten years, and during these periods of solitude there were revealed to me things innumerable and unfathomable. This much I shall say about that in order that others may be helped: I learnt with certainty that it is above all the mystics who walk on the road of God; their life is the best life, their method the soundest method, their character the purest character . . ..

In general, then, how is a mystic 'way' (*tariqah*) described? The purity which is the first condition of it is the purification of the heart completely from what is other than God; the key to it, which corresponds to the opening act of adoration in prayer, is the sinking of the heart completely in the recollection of God; and the end of it is complete absorption (*fana'*) in God.

Al-Ghazali, *Deliverance from Error*, tr. W. Montgomery Watt.

Counsel

Accept none other for thy love but God.
All things apart from Him are pure illusion.
Here is my counsel, if thou canst counsel take.
The rememberers are ever absent in their Beloved,
For none have life save those who are near to Him.
Between such and the Truth there is no veil.
What are the blessings of Paradise to them?
Passion God's slaves have melted; they have drunk,
And still drink, this eternal-treasured wine,
The draught whereof hath robbed them of themselves.
Would thou couldst take one sip out of their cup!
'Twould help to bridge the gap twixt thee and me.
A good slave he who saith: 'I am at Thy service',
Hearing God's Call which I address to him.
If God thou seekest, then companion me:
For thee, be very sure, there is no way else.

Shaykh Ahmad al-Alawi, *Diwan*.
Cited by Martin Lings, *A Sufi Saint of the Twentieth Century*